Leadership Coaching

From personal insight to organisational performance

Graham Lee is Director of Coaching at OCG Limited, a business psychology consultancy. His pioneering approach to coaching, developed over the last decade, draws on his extensive training and experience as a psychotherapist, as well as his business experience as a manager within the pharmaceutical industry. He coaches senior managers, provides supervision to groups of coaches, and is also a lecturer and conference speaker.

Leadership coaching has become a key to success for both individuals and organisations. Graham Lee demonstrates here that he is a master of the field, packing his book with insights and practical ideas. No one has done a better job of integrating our understandings from psychology into the training of today's leaders. I enthusiastically recommend this book to managers, coaches, therapists and students.

David Gergen
Director, Center for Public Leadership
John F Kennedy School, Harvard University and Former Adviser to Four US Presidents

A wise and thought provoking account of professional coaching. Graham Lee invites us to look more deeply at managerial motivations, and shows how coaching can guide the process of increasing self-awareness and creating lasting change.

The model of authentic leadership is particularly useful; I could immediately recognise how colleagues fit within it, and so understand the psychological journey that coaching will need to entail.

Stuart Horwood
Managing Director, BT Wholesale Markets

A book for all those looking for the answers to leadership coaching. This book offers unique insight into how to coach the individual whilst recognising the needs of the organisation.

Rising to the challenge of 'authentic leadership' the author provides the reassurances and the guides to address change through personal exploration and psychological challenge whilst addressing organisational goals – an essential read for those wishing to develop their employees.

Anne Watts, CBE
Head of Workplace and Diversity, Business in the Community

This is the book on coaching for leadership that takes the task deeper than any other that I have read, without losing the non-specialist reader. If you thought that you needed to know about countertransference and projective identification, but did not see yourself as going all the way to becoming psychotherapist or analyst, then this is the book for you. It is elegantly written, with plenty of case studies, and the relevance to coaching of every concept is clearly discussed. If you are going to read just one book on coaching this year, this is the one.

David Megginson, Professor of HRD, Sheffield Hallam University and co-chair
European Mentoring & Coaching Council.

The Chartered Institute of Personnel and Development is the leading publisher of books and reports for personnel and training professionals, students, and all those concerned with the effective management and development of people at work. For details of all our titles, please contact the Publishing Department:

tel. 020-8612 6204
e-mail publish@cipd.co.uk
The catalogue of all CIPD titles can be viewed on the CIPD website:
www.cipd.co.uk/bookstore

Leadership Coaching:

From personal insight to organisational performance

Graham Lee

Chartered Institute of Personnel and Development

Published by the Chartered Institute of Personnel and Development,
151 The Broadway, London SW19 1JQ

First published 2003
Reprinted 2005, 2006 (twice)

Design by Beacon GDT, Mitcheldean, Gloucestershire
Typeset by Fakenham Photosetting Ltd, Fakenham, Norfolk
Printed in Great Britain by The Cromwell Press, Trowbridge, Wiltshire

British Library Cataloguing in Publication Data
A catalogue of this publication is available from the British Library

ISBN 0 85292 996 x
ISBN-13 978 0 85292 996 4

The views expressed in this publication are the author's own and may not necessarily
reflect those of the CIPD.

The CIPD has made every effort to trace and acknowledge copyright holders. If any
source has been overlooked, CIPD Enterprises would be pleased to redress this
for future editions.

Chartered Institute of Personnel and Development, 151 The Broadway, London SW19 1JQ
Tel: 020 8612 6200
E-mail: cipd@cipd.co.uk Website: www.cipd.co.uk
Incorporated by Royal Charter. Registered Charity No. 1079797.

Contents

List of figures

List of tables

List of case studies

Acknowledgements

There are many people I wish to thank for their knowing or unknowing contribution to this book. First, I wish to thank my colleagues at OCG Limited, Arabella Ellis, Gill Gustar, Mark Loftus, Lou Wilcock, and Charlie Worters for their willingness to listen, engage, offer ideas, and to make useful comments. I also wish to thank all those coaches and therapists that I have worked with for their insight and wisdom. In particular I wish to acknowledge the invaluable feedback on early drafts provided by Liz Pick and Claire Leggatt. My thanks also to the numerous managers that I have had the privilege of working with, and whose determination to engage with a more authentic style has made the coaching enterprise so inspiring for me.

My thanks also to Cameron and Madeline, my children, for being themselves and for giving me space to be myself. Finally, I wish to dedicate the book to my parents, Helga and David Lee.

Introduction

We do not receive wisdom, we must discover it for ourselves . . .

Marcel Proust (1871–1922)

Leadership coaching is concerned with enabling managers to change. It has developed as a method for providing managers at all levels with the essential space to reflect. Through reflection, managers come to understand themselves more fully, to confront their obstacles and concerns, to nurture their drives and aspirations, and ultimately to release and channel their creativity towards their organisational goals. Grounded in the development of personal and interpersonal awareness, leadership coaching encourages managers to challenge self-limiting mindsets and to stretch for possibilities that might previously have seemed out of reach.

However, such change is not easily evoked. Even if managers are motivated to change and develop, problematic patterns of being and relating can be powerfully persistent. They may try to adopt new approaches or techniques, but can find themselves reverting to their habitual styles after a week or two, resigning themselves to the idea that certain behaviours are part of their personalities, or reassuring themselves that they can continue to be successful despite certain shortcomings. Resistance to change is part and parcel of being human, and if coaching is to be successful, it must engage with the unconscious resistance that managers have to change, as well as their conscious intentions and determination. It needs to evoke a depth of personal understanding that enables them to see how their habitual styles and preferences have developed, and to use this awareness as a platform for defining and realising new possibilities.

Stepping into the realm of the personal

This perspective on leadership coaching, with its emphasis on the personal awareness that underpins sustainable change, contrasts with the approach adopted by many coaches. The rapid rise in coaching has seen many people offering their services as coaches based primarily on their prior business experience. The emphasis in their style of coaching is on sharing their experiences and cultivating specific competencies – but there is usually a rigid avoidance of personal or psychological issues. Such boundaries are entirely appropriate for coaches who are not qualified to delve more deeply into the motivations of managers. Indeed, if they do stumble upon emotionally-charged underlying issues, they can quickly find themselves out of their depth.

Yet limiting the domain of coaching to those issues that are tangibly relevant to business performance places it within a straitjacket, and for many managers, forecloses on its capacity to evoke significant change. Although not all coaching need necessarily step into the realm of the personal, for many managers this is precisely where coaching ought to go. To evoke the mix of authenticity, creativity, interpersonal competence, and influential impact that is the overarching goal of leadership coaching, its scope must straddle personal and organisational domains.

Only by stepping into the realm of the personal – by engaging managers in the relationship between their individual drives and business goals, their blind spots and their development needs – can coaching harness the passions and convictions that underpin leadership excellence.

The psychological dimension in coaching

It is a central premise of this book that, for many managers, to achieve significant, sustainable, and organisationally relevant change, leadership coaching must encompass personal and psychological issues, as well as practical issues. This expansion in scope challenges coaches to be more sophisticated in their understanding of psychology. They need to develop skills and experience that enable them to move more freely between the psychological and the practical. They need to understand a wider range of theoretical models and frameworks, and to be able to relate psychological insights to business performance.

The experience and expertise of coaches offering their services to organisations is highly variable. Whereas some coaches have a grounding and training in business and one-to-one development, many set up as coaches with relatively little experience (Cribbs, 2002; Williams, 2001). At best this means that coaching is limited in its effectiveness. At worst, it means that issues are stirred up in managers that coaches are not qualified to handle, or that problematic behaviours in managers become reinforced rather than transformed (Berglas, 2002). For leadership coaching to be more reliably effective there is a need for greater sophistication on the part of both sponsors and coaches.

Sponsors of coaching – typically human resource professionals or line managers – must be more discriminating in their choice of coaches, and must select those who have the right portfolio of skills to work with a wider scope of issues (Cribbs, 2002). Coaches need to undertake training and ongoing supervision that deepens their personal and psychological awareness alongside their organisational knowledge. In my view coaches do not have to be qualified psychologists or psychotherapists, but they do need experience and training that cultivates a depth of psychological-mindedness, as well as business-mindedness. (This is discussed in detail in Chapter 9.)

THE AIMS OF THE BOOK

This book demonstrates how leadership coaching can be more psychological, while retaining a practical focus on performance improvement.

I present an approach to coaching that draws on psychotherapeutic concepts. The aim is to show how coaches can blend psychological and business concepts, using them to enhance understanding and so help managers achieve sustainable change. A complementary aim is to illustrate to sponsors the kinds of psychological issues that coaching should embrace in order to facilitate useful change and development.

Structuring frameworks

A psychological approach to coaching does not have to be impenetrable. Although some of the concepts I discuss are complex, their usefulness depends on their accessibility. For this reason I have structured the book around two complementary frameworks, both of which are denoted by a mnemonic:

- the ACE FIRST model of change, and
- the LASER coaching process.

The ACE FIRST model of change is a framework for making sense of patterns of doing, thinking and feeling (Actions, Cognitions and Emotions), and the impact of organisational context on these patterns. This model enables coaches and sponsors to understand the range of information that has to be considered when working with the personal, practical and organisational aspects of change.

The LASER coaching process represents the journey of coaching in five stages (Learning, Assessing, Story-making, Enabling, and Reframing). I work through each of these stages in detail, highlighting the kinds of skills that coaches require and the kinds of issues that are likely to arise in relation to sponsors or managers.

KEY THEMES

Within the context of the ACE FIRST model of change, and the LASER coaching process, there are a number of important themes that run through the book. I draw attention to three key themes:

- the notion of authentic leadership as the goal of leadership coaching
- the need to acknowledge unconscious factors in influencing potential change
- the need for coaches to hold in mind multiple perspectives.

Evoking authentic leadership

The overarching aim of leadership coaching is the development of authentic leadership. I define authentic leadership in relation to two defensive forms of leadership – defiant leadership and compliant leadership – and I refer to these characteristic styles throughout the book. I use these concepts to illustrate typical development challenges that many managers face, and show how an understanding of these styles indicates the kinds of coaching interventions that are likely to be effective.

Acknowledging unconscious factors

A second theme in the book concerns the role of the unconscious. Unconscious issues, and in particular the emotional factors that underpin unconscious motivations, exert a profound impact on the ability of managers to change, and yet they are aspects that are not usually addressed within coaching. I show how unconscious resistance to change is one of the factors that coaches need to address, and discuss approaches to the unconscious at different stages of the coaching process.

Holding multiple perspectives

A third theme concerns the need for a coach to be able to hold multiple perspectives in mind and to view challenges and issues from different viewpoints. Underpinning this concept is the view that there is no single truth about what enables a manager to change, but rather a series of constructions that is more or less useful for evoking change. To work flexibly with different managers, moving between personal and organisational issues, and examining conscious and unconscious factors, coaches must be able to shift their focus of attention, to entertain alternative hypotheses, and to adapt their approach to different situations.

WHO IS THE BOOK FOR?

This book is addressed to three primary groups of people:

- coaches, and those wishing to train as a coach
- sponsors of coaching
- managers who are receiving coaching.

Coaches

For coaches and training coaches there is a need for a model of coaching that brings together psychotherapeutic ideas in a way that is accessible and relevant to leadership coaching. The book provides an integration that draws on the major schools of psychotherapy. It demonstrates how these concepts can be used to gain insight about the developmental challenge facing managers, and how insights can be translated into interventions that evoke practical change.

Sponsors

Sponsors play a central role in the use of coaching in organisations, from the initial assessment of the need for coaching, through the selection and engagement of coaches, to the management and final evaluation of the process. As coaching becomes more widely available, sponsors have to be better informed about different approaches to coaching and their appropriateness for different development challenges. This book provides sponsors with an accessible introduction to the deeper psychological issues that underpin performance, and shows how these can be effectively addressed within leadership coaching.

There is also a consideration of the competencies necessary for effective coaching, and a process for buying coaching services.

Managers

For managers who are either in the process of selecting a coach or already receiving coaching, the book provides a resource to understand the journey they are undertaking. It provides a picture of the kinds of exploration they can expect, and indicates how personal issues can be handled in relation to business goals.

AN OUTLINE OF THE BOOK

The first three chapters set the scene for leadership coaching. Chapter 1 explores what I describe as *the paradox of leadership* and the particular challenge of coaching to enable managers to display authentic leadership. I discuss the journey of coaching, and the need for this journey to explore personal and practical issues. In light of the emphasis on the personal journey, I also discuss the relationship between coaching and therapy, and distinguish coaching in terms of its organisational goals.

Chapter 2 presents *the ACE FIRST model of change*, describes each of the factors within this model, and illustrates the use of the model with case studies.

Chapter 3 turns to *the role of the unconscious* in leadership coaching. I consider the role of psychoanalytic theory in making sense of unconscious agendas, and in particular, draw on attachment theory as a model for understanding the impact of early experiences on leadership style.

The next five chapters, Chapters 4 to 8, present the successive stages of the LASER coaching process. Chapter 4 discusses *the development of the learning space* and the qualities of the relationship between coach and manager that are required to create and sustain this reflective space.

Chapter 5 – *Assessing* – considers how coaches gather information, the different sources of information, and the use of different types of question to guide the process of discovery. I also consider attitudes to change and the particular ways in which resistance to change can become manifest.

Chapter 6 – *Story-making* – explores how the information gathered during the Assessing stage is used to construct useful stories about the development challenge facing managers. Five types of story are described which draw on different elements of the ACE FIRST framework.

Chapter 7 – *Enabling* – considers the factors that can promote or limit change according to the coach's assessment of the development challenge.

Chapter 8 – *Reframing* – describes the interventions that coaches make to evoke change. The chapter also addresses the conscious and unconscious issues that must be considered in relation to the ending of coaching.

The final chapter, Chapter 9, considers the competencies and training required for effective coaching.

Questionnaires and worksheets to support the frameworks presented in this book are available at www.ocg.co.uk.

Terminology

I refer throughout to those receiving coaching as 'managers', regardless of their specific position within an organisation. The term 'sponsor' refers to the person who holds the budget for coaching. Where managers refer themselves for coaching, they are both sponsor and manager.

Some commentators and practitioners draw various distinctions between the terms 'coaching' and 'mentoring', but there appears to be little consensus about such distinctions. I have used the term 'coaching' to refer to the one-to-one development of managers at all levels of organisations, whether that development takes place over a short or longer period of time, and whether the stated focus of change is primarily personal or organisational.

A number of case studies have been used to illustrate the ideas presented in this book. These case studies are drawn from my own work as a leadership coach, from the work of my colleagues, and from my work as a supervisor of other coaches. The identity of managers has been disguised to maintain confidentiality.

1

The challenge of authentic leadership

This above all: to thine own self be true.

Hamlet, I, iii, 78

Coaching is arguably the most powerful method for developing managers' capacity for leadership. From junior to senior managers, organisations need individuals who can shape and realise success, drawing on their ability to influence, inspire, collaborate, manage and above all, lead. The challenge of developing such qualities is that they cannot be simply learned from a textbook or workshop. If leadership is to be truly effective, managers must be authentic. Their acts of influence must be grounded in self-awareness, confidence and creativity, and their engagement with others must empower and motivate. The development of such qualities demands that managers develop their self-understanding.

Leadership coaching is uniquely placed to draw out the individual qualities of managers, and to help them to connect their talents productively to the achievement of organisational goals. Whether the goal is to strengthen interpersonal skills, to build team effectiveness, to enhance influence and impact, or to help managers to adapt quickly to a new role, it is through the reflective environment of leadership coaching that individual qualities can be most effectively nurtured. By engaging with the individual at a personal level, as well as with their skills and capabilities, coaching can take on the challenge of evoking what I describe as authentic leadership.

In this chapter I explore the challenge of authentic leadership in terms of the paradox between the personal and the organisational, and describe the overarching goal of leadership coaching as having to work with this essential paradox. I contrast authentic leadership with two other forms of leadership – defiant leadership and compliant leadership – and consider the significance of them in terms of the performance of managers. These different types of leadership, and the psychological factors associated with them, provide a framework for understanding the task of leadership coaching.

Against this backdrop I describe the journey of leadership coaching, and in particular the need to work with the personal as well as the practical aspects of change. I end the chapter by considering the relationship between coaching and therapy, and show that coaching is distinguished in terms of its dual emphasis on personal and organisational goals.

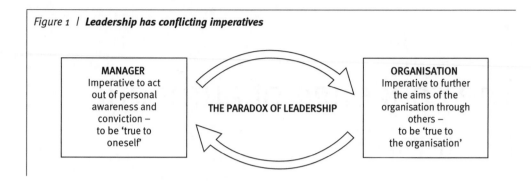

Figure 1 | *Leadership has conflicting imperatives*

THE PARADOX OF LEADERSHIP

In one respect effective leadership stems from managers being attuned with their core values, from reaching inside for the authority that comes from personal awareness and conviction. To this extent effective leadership must contain a fundamental individuality. However, in another respect, leadership is fundamentally concerned with the collective – with others and the organisation. It focuses on the agreed purposes and strategies of the organisation and is concerned with influencing others to achieve group goals.

Effective leadership thus contains two potentially conflicting imperatives. On the one hand is the imperative for the manager to be 'true to oneself', to act out of personal awareness and conviction. On the other hand is the imperative for the manager to be 'true to the organisation', to act in ways that meet the needs of the organisation through others. These potentially conflicting needs form the poles of a paradox – the paradox of leadership (see Figure 1).

It could be argued that sometimes a manager's individual drives are perfectly aligned with those of the organisation, that there is no tension or paradox between the personal and the organisational. Such an idea is as appealing as that of romantic love, where the needs and desires of one person are perfectly matched to the needs and desires of another. But

Table 1 | *Tensions between personal and organisational needs*

Personal need/drive	Organisational need/drive
Demonstrate ability to understand and motivate others.	*Get tasks done and produce results.*
Establish a better work–life balance.	*Find and keep highly committed people.*
Draw on ability to network and develop relationships.	*Promote those who can think strategically.*
Make a difference to other people's lives.	*Increase market share and profitability.*
Express passion about environmental issues.	*Profit comes first – just keep the right side of environmental lobbies.*

as we all know, this is an ideal. To sustain a real relationship takes conscious effort. In the world of real managers exerting influence in real organisations there is always a tension between managers' needs and motives and those of the organisation, or at a more immediate level, between managers and the individuals or groups they are seeking to influence.

Examples of tensions between the personal and the organisational are shown in Table 1.

AUTHENTIC LEADERSHIP

The most effective leadership is the result of managers' being able to sustain the tension between personal goals and those of the organisation, and finding a conscious and creative solution that can arise out of the paradox of leadership.[1] It is based on matching individual expression to organisational need, and is creative in the sense that the needs neither of the individual nor of the organisation are sacrificed (see Figure 1).

Authenticity implies someone whose whole way of being, doing and relating is concordant with his or her beliefs and values. It implies a real depth of awareness about himself or herself, and a willingness and capacity to say things openly and boldly. Most of us can relate to the idea of authenticity – the hope or experience that our talents and drives are being expressed in our work lives; that the attunement between our abilities and what we do, will yield success and appropriate rewards.

But for the manager seeking to influence others, personal authenticity is not enough. Authenticity must be connected with the need to guide others in their actions or opinions in a way that is attuned to the organisation. The success of authentic leadership is that it carries personal conviction *and* attunement with the organisation. Managers' efforts to influence others are more motivational, more inspirational, and more practically useful because their authentic behaviours and communications are concordant with the values and expectations of the organisation.

The creativity in authentic leadership is evident in the solutions that managers develop to address the tensions between personal and organisational needs. Authentic leadership

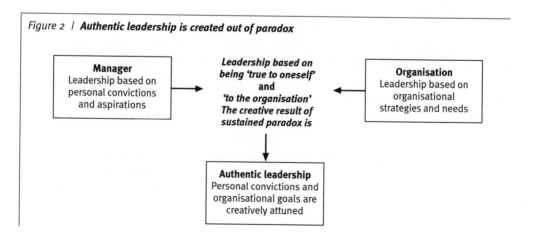

*Figure 2 | **Authentic leadership is created out of paradox***

Table 2 | The creative possibilities of authentic leadership

Personal need/drive	Possibilities arising from sustaining paradox	Organisational need/drive
Demonstrate ability to understand and motivate others.	*Lead a project to show that relationship development can have a direct impact on better results.*	*Get tasks done and produce results.*
Establish a better work–life balance.	*Form a network of part-time workers in order to provide greater flexibility and resource savings for the organisation.*	*Find and keep highly committed people.*
Draw on ability to network and develop relationships.	*Influence senior managers to value networking and strategic thinking by showing that a strategy will be more successful if supported with buy-in gained through networking.*	*Promote those who can think strategically.*
Make a difference to other people's lives.	*Understand what is most important to customers, and lead developments to meet these needs.*	*Increase market share and profitability.*
Express passion about environmental issues.	*Lead the organisation's environmental policy and use this as an important marketing message.*	*Profit comes first.*

does not imply making a compromise in which neither personal nor organisational goals are fully satisfied, but rather implies shaping new possibilities for individuals and for the organisation (see Table 2).

Authentic leadership is conscious leadership

The challenge of authentic leadership is that it demands awareness – self-awareness, awareness of others and organisational awareness. Such awareness provides the basis for conscious leadership, by which managers are able to examine their motives and make conscious judgements. Furthermore, they are able to identify unhelpful defences or reactions in themselves – perhaps a tendency to control or dominate based on a fear of failure; perhaps a fear of conflict and a desire to appease; perhaps an excessive competitiveness that leads to distrust; perhaps a tendency to be insular in such a way as to seem detached and uninspiring.

Self-awareness enables managers to identify personal drives that are less distorted by unconscious bias. In authentic leadership this self-awareness is coupled to an awareness of others, curiosity about what motivates others, a capacity to understand and value the differences between self and others, and an awareness of how motivations of individuals, groups and teams can be harnessed to the goals of the organisation. Authentic leadership achieved through the sustaining of paradox depends on conscious awareness.

CASE STUDY

Roger

Roger was a senior manager in a major pharmaceutical company, with global responsibility for the product licensing strategy. Roger was charged with licensing one or more products from other companies. However, despite the identification of a number of potential licensing compounds, on three previous occasions the company had failed to persuade the licenser to go ahead with them. On each occasion the licenser had chosen a competitor.

During this time Roger was receiving leadership coaching. He used the coaching to examine how his conscious leadership could have a more positive impact on the licensing of a new compound. He recognised that he was good at networking inside and outside the organisation, and that he evoked strong team loyalty. However, in his role as a strategic director he felt that the organisation expected him to be an outstanding strategist, and he had learned to behave as if this capability was a genuine strength. He had worked hard at writing his own strategy papers, and for the 'pitch' to prospective licensers he had slaved over his marketing presentations. Members of his team were not invited to contribute to the wider strategic pitch. In his leadership, Roger was trying to conform to the organisation's need for a strategic leader, and was losing sight of his genuine strengths. Furthermore, he was failing to achieve the organisation's goal of licensing a new compound.

Leadership coaching enabled Roger to develop his self-awareness. He realised that he had built his ambition on the belief that to be a leader he would have to be a visionary. He had denied to himself the thought that strategic creativity was not one of his strengths, and had unwittingly excluded other team members from helping to develop his strategies. Through coaching he realised that he needed to play to his authentic strengths – to use his motivational skills to harness the creativity of his team in developing the strategic story. Then he could use his excellent interpersonal, networking and presentation skills to bring together the diverse stakeholders within his company, and to co-ordinate a more coherent and convincing case for a licenser. When he did this for the next licensing compound that became available, his company won the contract. Furthermore, Roger was widely acknowledged to have been the architect of the successful licensing deal.

DEFENSIVE OR REACTIVE FORMS OF LEADERSHIP

Many managers do not possess the awareness of self and others that is necessary for authentic leadership. Their leadership style is unconsciously shaped by their personal biases: their implicit mindsets, automatic reactions and defences based on past experiences. These biases are not necessarily bad – indeed, they have usually contributed to their achievements. For instance, a manager driven to succeed due to a competitive upbringing can be highly valued in any organisation that needs an unswerving achievement-focus. However, the limitation to such leadership comes from its lack of flexibility. Without awareness there is no basis for making choices about how to lead according to circumstance. There is no perspective for examining personal motives and holding them in tension with organisational needs and challenges.

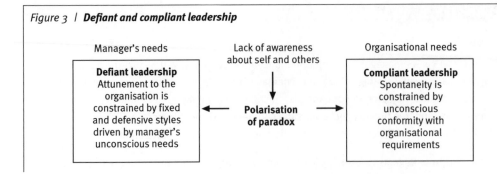

Figure 3 | *Defiant and compliant leadership*

Manager's needs

Lack of awareness about self and others

Organisational needs

Defiant leadership
Attunement to the organisation is constrained by fixed and defensive styles driven by manager's unconscious needs

Polarisation of paradox

Compliant leadership
Spontaneity is constrained by unconscious conformity with organisational requirements

A manager's lack of awareness of self and others leads to an unconscious polarisation of the paradox of leadership, a collapsing of the tension between individual needs and organisational needs (see Figure 3). The direction of this polarisation, either towards the manager's personal agenda or towards the organisational agenda, gives rise to two defensive forms of leadership: defiant leadership and compliant leadership.

DEFIANT LEADERSHIP

Defiant leadership occurs when there is a collapse of the paradox towards the manager's personal needs. These personal needs are unconscious, or there is an attempt to ignore or disguise personal doubts and uncertainties. This style of leadership is defiant in the sense that the manager behaves in a way that implicitly says, 'This is me, so take it or leave it.' There is minimal accommodation of his or her needs to those of the organisation. Underpinning defiant leadership is a fear of failure, or a guardedness about admitting to vulnerability, and these unconscious fears are rooted in the manager's past experiences.

You can probably think of managers in organisations whose style of leadership is defiant. They have risen to senior levels as a result of their energy and apparent strength of personal conviction. Their leadership style is powerful to the extent that it is underpinned by their unconscious personal agendas, and they are driven to impose their view of what needs to be done on others. However, their leadership is limited because they are unaware of, or ignore, the impact they have on others. They are commonly experienced as controlling, and tend to evoke competitiveness, resistance or unimaginative obedience. Defiant leadership is ineffective to the extent that it fails to evoke the voluntary creativity and excellence of others.

Defiant leadership and personality

Personality profiles are sometimes used as an excuse for a manager's defiant leadership. For example, a manager may use the information from a personality test which indicates a propensity to control others in an extrovert and structured way, as proof that his or her behaviour is inevitable – as if authenticity was simply being true to his or her personality profile regardless of consequences. In leadership coaching a personality profile can be very useful, since it provides a basis for managers to understand their preferred styles.

However, authentic leadership demands that this personal awareness be held in tension with an understanding of one's own impact on others, and a consideration of how this impact helps or hinders the achievement of organisational goals. Awareness about personality preferences provides a basis for choice rather than a vindication of behaviour regardless of impact.

CASE STUDY

Elizabeth

Elizabeth was head of business development in an international company operating within a thriving service industry. She was a highly successful salesperson and was competent at managing her extensive network of external contacts. However, her relationships with her colleagues and team members were strained. Although she was valued for her energy, determination and business acumen, interpersonally they found her abrasive and dismissive. She had received substantial feedback through the years about her development needs, and had attended interpersonal skills training courses. However, she did not really believe she needed to change, and would blame her colleagues for being too sensitive. She had achieved her success by being tough and individualistic and was strongly resistant to change, even though the chief executive was doubtful about promoting her onto the board. The career success she had achieved through her defiant leadership was now limiting her further progress.

COMPLIANT LEADERSHIP

At the other extreme there can be a polarisation of the paradox towards the requirements of the organisation. In this case the manager works to develop the knowledge, skills and competencies that are valued by the organisation. This style of leadership is compliant in the sense that managers have learned to suppress unconsciously their natural styles and qualities in an attempt to be what they perceive the organisation wants from its leaders. This suppression of personal authenticity is learned through experiences of needing to accommodate to others in the past. Managers who show compliant leadership have often risen to middle and senior management positions where they are considered to be steady and reliable – a 'safe pair of hands'. They are well attuned to the present needs of the organisation, responding effectively to challenges and supporting the status quo. However, an apparent lack of spontaneity can limit their leadership. The suppression of their personal preferences can result in a kind of competent blandness, manifesting as a failure to motivate others, or a lack of imagination in their approach to new problems.

Compliant leadership and management

The skills and qualities required for effective leadership are often distinguished from those required for effective management. Whereas leadership is concerned with inspiring and influencing others, management is concerned with planning, organising, directing and controlling. Compliant leadership is similar to effective management, where the supervision and direction of effective routines is maintained. If a manager is working with a group of highly motivated staff whose personal needs are closely aligned with those of the organisation, and where existing procedures are effective, the need for authentic leadership is at a minimum. In this circumstance compliant leadership may be adequate. But if there is a need to develop new approaches, to motivate staff, or to respond to changing circumstances, then there is also a need for authentic leadership.

CASE STUDY

Peter

Peter was an experienced manager who, following a merger, had been appointed to, and had chaired, a senior executive team. His maturity of style and gravitas suited the role, and he enjoyed co-ordinating the contributions of his fellow directors, following up on agreed actions, and reporting regularly to the chief executive. However, after a year in the role there was a reshuffle and Peter found himself left out of the executive team. Peter's demotion was a result of his compliant leadership. Although he was considered efficient and productive in the role, he had failed to inject the urgency, passion and determination necessary to meet the challenges of the organisation at that time. The organisation needed to become revitalised. To achieve that it required a quality of leadership that was less constrained by the established protocols of the past.

DEVELOPING AUTHENTIC LEADERSHIP

Developing authentic leadership is one of the key challenges facing organisations. If an organisation is to shape and respond to its circumstances, it needs leadership throughout the organisation that carries the wisdom of consciousness. The responsibility for the development of an organisation's leadership potential usually lies with human resource professionals, who seek to match the need for training and development to the strategic direction and resourcing needs of the organisation.

I have found it useful to distinguish targets for management development by considering two dimensions – whether the development is people- or task-focused, and whether the goal is individual or organisational development (see Figure 4).

On the task side, individual managers need core *skills and capabilities* to perform their role (top right quadrant), which include such attributes as communication skills, team management skills and business knowledge. If managers take on a *business leadership* role (bottom right quadrant), their tasks are more concerned with wider organisational issues, such as the setting of strategic direction and managing complexity.

The people-focus side of this model resembles the components of emotional intelligence (Salovey *et al*, 1990; Goleman, 1996). For the individual, the primary need is for *self-awareness* (top left quadrant), which includes knowing and managing one's own emotions, and harnessing those emotions to achieve desired goals. At the team or organisational level, the need is for *motivational leadership* (bottom left quadrant), which includes understanding and developing others and managing relationships effectively.

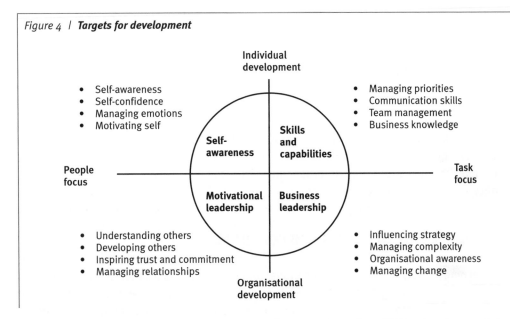

Figure 4 | *Targets for development*

The development of authentic leadership needs to encompass all four quadrants of this model. For example, if a person is to exhibit effective communication skills or to handle conflict as part of his or her team management (top right), he or she will have to be able to manage his or her emotions (top left). If a manager is to influence the strategic direction of the organisation (bottom right), he or she must be able to understand others and to manage relationships effectively (bottom left). The challenge for human resource professionals is to identify for an individual or group of managers both what the development need is, and the most appropriate means to facilitate that development.

THE BIAS TOWARDS TASK

In organisations it is common to focus on the task aspects of change, at the expense of the personal aspects. This bias is understandable to the extent that organisations need to respond quickly to market changes. When there is pressure to achieve something, managers look for tangible solutions, and when people need to be developed, the aim is to get them to produce useful results as quickly as possible. In a context of urgency, accountability and measurable performance, dwelling on the people-focused aspects of change can seem like a luxury.

For example, although competency frameworks and 360-degree feedback exercises usually contain items for so-called 'soft' skills, such as 'motivating others', and 'managing relationships effectively', less attention is paid to these if a manager has delivered the 'hard' business results. It may be that in delivering those results the manager has created difficult working relationships, but many organisations turn a blind eye to such failings while the manager continues to contribute to profit. In the short term this may seem like the right business decision, but in the long run such a manager will undermine the performance of others, and ultimately the organisation.

The increasing interest in emotional intelligence indicates recognition that the competencies of 'self-awareness' and 'managing relationships effectively' are fundamental aspects of effective leadership. However, even emotional intelligence is in danger of becoming yet another set of capabilities that are imposed on an individual. The problem with imposed skills is that they are not assimilated as real learning, and usually disappear as soon as the manager is put under pressure. Thus, for example, managers who have learned to ask open questions and to value the ideas of others, are viewed by colleagues as 'just going through the motions' if the managers become dismissive of others as soon as they need to get something done quickly. Such inconsistencies in behaviour breed distrust, and interpersonal skills can be viewed as a kind of political correctness or a hoop to jump through to get the right kind of peer review. There can be a façade of compliant leadership that in fact disguises a more defiant leadership style.

THE PROBLEM OF TASK-FOCUSED COACHING

Individual coaching is one of the options available for the development of managers. It has become widely used in organisations to provide a more tailored developmental experience, particularly for senior and middle managers. However, coaching can sometimes fall into exactly the same trap as other management development interventions where the primary focus is on the development of skills. Such a bias towards skills, in preference to the development of consciousness and self-knowledge, discourages the development of authentic leadership. The skills and competencies needed to perform management tasks take precedence over the use of coaching as a space for reflection and discovery, and as a consequence tend to evoke either compliant or defiant leadership. Either managers seek to comply with set learning tasks, in the belief that this will enable them to fit better with the leadership needs of the organisation, or they disregard the learning in a defiant way, privately believing that they will continue to be effective if they stick to their established styles.

CASE STUDY

Alan

Alan, the chief executive of a multinational organisation, chose to appoint a coach soon after a company merger. He viewed the purpose of coaching as providing him with a sounding-board at a time when he had to make a number of important decisions. The coach he appointed was a man who had previously worked at board level within his industry, and who had been a successful businessman in his own right. The coach was useful to Alan to the extent that he provided a space in which Alan could air his thoughts. However, Alan's primary concern was that morale amongst senior managers following the merger was low, and business was beginning to suffer. Some managers had hinted to Alan that his critical and controlling style was not helping, and indeed two senior people had decided to leave. Alan had succeeded as a defiant leader, but was now finding that his leadership style was creating problems.

CASE STUDY continued

Alan sensed that he needed to become more motivational as a leader and explored this idea with his coach. However, his coach – whose own business experience was as a driving leader – unwittingly encouraged Alan to focus on his business leadership goals, to set ever more challenging targets, and to punish dissent with critical feedback. His coach reinforced Alan's defiant leadership style. Alan failed to make the appropriate change because his coach's skills and experience were misaligned with his development need. Alan needed leadership coaching aimed at developing his authentic leadership.

LEADERSHIP COACHING

The purpose of leadership coaching is to develop authentic leadership – to enable managers to be more consciously aware, and so create a style of leadership that is both personally distinctive and organisationally attuned. To do this, leadership coaching must embrace the personal and the practical. Self-awareness must be connected with the practical actions and approaches that make change a reality. We can thus think of leadership coaching as providing a space for a double, parallel journey – a personal journey and a practical journey (see Figure 5; see also Wales, 2003).

The personal journey

It is usual to have a boundary between what is personal and what is public. There are things that we feel, think and do in our personal lives that we do not share at work, and sometimes not even with others outside work. In many situations, discretion about what we express or discuss at work is appropriate. However, the division between the personal

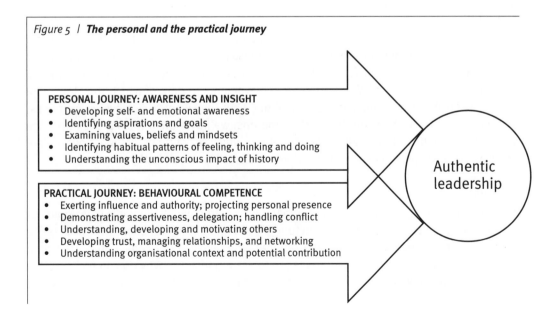

Figure 5 / *The personal and the practical journey*

PERSONAL JOURNEY: AWARENESS AND INSIGHT
- Developing self- and emotional awareness
- Identifying aspirations and goals
- Examining values, beliefs and mindsets
- Identifying habitual patterns of feeling, thinking and doing
- Understanding the unconscious impact of history

PRACTICAL JOURNEY: BEHAVIOURAL COMPETENCE
- Exerting influence and authority; projecting personal presence
- Demonstrating assertiveness, delegation; handling conflict
- Understanding, developing and motivating others
- Developing trust, managing relationships, and networking
- Understanding organisational context and potential contribution

Authentic leadership

self and the business self can be extreme, and is often reinforced by the cultural norms within an organisation. The people in leadership roles, at different levels of an organisation, model these norms. There are explicit and implicit norms: explicit team norms invariably include 'being open', 'being honest', 'being collaborative', 'listening', and 'challenging'. However, there are also implicit norms, which might include 'not being too open', 'not showing your emotions', 'not being uncomfortably candid' and 'not being too different'. These implicit norms – which are often more powerful than explicit ones because they operate outside conscious choice – mean that feelings are hidden or ignored.

When managers embark on coaching, they transfer their norms about the work environment to the coaching environment. They expect coaching conversations to proceed in a similar way to appraisal and development discussions with their boss. Further, there are many coaches who also operate within these norms, providing a sounding-board for the manager about work issues, but not encouraging discussions to roam more widely. One of the first tasks of leadership coaching is to establish new norms for the coaching context. The coaching space must be one in which conversations can be, at least in part, deeply personal.

At this stage I highlight three areas of conversation that must be established as permissible territory within the personal journey. These are

- aspirations
- emotions
- history.

Each of these aspects is discussed in more detail in subsequent chapters.

Aspirations

Amidst the pressure to get things done managers can lose sight of their personal aspirations. Why did they choose to go into business in the first place? What did they hope to achieve for themselves or for others? Who are their role models, and in what ways do they wish to emulate them? What are their achievements to date of which they feel most proud? By encouraging managers to think about what they want to achieve in their lives, rather than in their work within the next six months, we invite them to step back from the day-to-day turmoil, and to recall those aspirations which make them feel most passionate and alive. (The shaping of aspirations and intentions is discussed further in Chapter 2.)

Emotions

A senior director of a multinational company was extremely challenging to a group of consultants about a proposed restructure of the marketing function. He was being aggressive and refused to listen to the rational arguments of the consultants. He was a bully. Eventually a junior consultant managed to ask a question: 'Why do you feel that this proposed structure won't work?' He rounded on the consultant: 'Don't bring feelings into this!'

I was that junior consultant, and reflecting later about this bruising meeting I was struck by his comment. Despite the fact that his response to our proposal was overwhelmingly emotional – his feelings were dominating the meeting – he attacked me for saying 'Why do you feel ...?' rather than 'Why do you think ... ?' It was as if emotions were puny things that simply get in the way of business decision-making. I later learned that this director had received a fierce dressing-down from his boss earlier in the day. I suspect he was feeling bullied himself, and consequently vented his feelings by bullying us.

What this experience taught me is that emotions can dominate behaviour, but are often denied – especially so in a business context.

Emotions lie at the heart of authentic leadership. Leaders who do not understand and manage their emotions will not be able to relate to others effectively; they will not be able to motivate others, or to make sense of why others are resisting their ideas or direction. In leadership coaching we need to establish emotions as an important area for discussion. Many managers are completely unfamiliar with the idea of identifying, naming and discussing their feelings, particularly those male managers who view emotions as a problematic attribute manifested mostly by women. However, learning to identify and make sense of emotions is a skill that can be learned. In coaching, managers come to learn how their emotions are directly linked with patterns of thinking and doing, and that managing emotions is a crucial part of achieving their goals.

History

Human beings are in many ways a product of their experiences. Whatever natural characteristics we are born with, we are powerfully shaped by our upbringing and other life experiences. In response to those experiences we develop distinctive patterns of being, feeling, thinking, relating and behaving. Whereas some aspects are part of our personality and likely to remain fairly stable throughout our lives, other aspects are more susceptible to change. In coaching we seek to understand how certain patterns of relating in the present have been formed through experience. In particular, we want to promote those patterns that help managers achieve their goals, and to discourage or replace those patterns that are damaging their relationships or are getting in the way of achieving their goals.

Most of us are unaware of how our patterns of experience define our ways of being in the present, in what subtle ways our styles are unconsciously tailored by the nuances and contingencies of our personal histories. An examination of personal history provides the coach, and managers being coached, with a means to identify those patterns that are effective, and others that are ineffective. The act of identifying such patterns, of making them conscious, allows managers to make a choice. Freed from the domain of conditioned response, managers are open to learn new behaviours – they are ready to connect the personal journey to the practical journey.

The practical journey

Awareness and insight, gained through the personal journey of coaching, are sometimes enough to help managers to initiate important changes, but usually the practical implications of new learning have to be translated more explicitly into new behaviours. Movement between the personal and practical journey is an important part of leadership coaching, because it parallels the need for managers to sustain an awareness of both personal and organisational goals. This linking of the personal and practical is part of the process of leadership coaching.

At this stage I highlight four aspects of the practical journey that help to ensure that change is achieved and sustained:

- practising new behaviours
- providing information
- action planning
- reviewing experiments.

Practising new behaviours

Learning to have different kinds of conversations is one of the most common outcomes from coaching. Whether managers are too aggressive or too passive, too verbose or too quiet, too funny or too serious, role-playing conversations with the coach can be a valuable opportunity to experiment with different styles and to receive immediate feedback. Typically, the coach will ask a manager to describe a real-life work scenario, and will play the role of one of the manager's colleagues or customers as the manager practises different approaches to the conversation. The greater the level of trust that the coach has established with the manager, the more willing he or she will be to take risks and to experiment with new styles.

Providing information

The need to practise new skills and behaviours can be usefully supported by articles, books, websites and handouts on specific management techniques. Popular examples include information on such areas as influence, delegation, negotiation, managing stress, emotional intelligence, relationship intelligence, managing teams, assertiveness, as well as resources to support psychometric test results, or for interpreting a 360-degree feedback report.

But although the use of such resources is valuable – particularly for those managers who enjoy reading and reflecting on their own – they can come to dominate coaching conversations. It is important for coaches to strike a balance between providing, on the one hand, useful inputs, and on the other, a space for open-ended reflection and personal discovery. It can be especially important when managers are fairly passive, and expect the coach to do all the work. This is usually a sign of resistance to change and must be addressed directly.

Action planning

If change is to be realised, it has to be turned into action – a change in behaviour, a change in thinking, a change in the way feelings are handled. For some people change follows readily from the discussion of an issue with a coach, but for others there is need for a more explicit plan of action. The plan serves as a commitment to change, and provides a basis for reviewing progress in subsequent sessions. As far as possible the plan is shaped by managers in response to questioning from the coach, defining *what* will be different *by when*, and identifying *how* managers will know if they have succeeded.

Reviewing experiments

One of the most common actions resulting from the practical journey of coaching is for managers to undertake an experiment in doing something different. Such experiments might be to try a different style of communication in a particular meeting, to plan a project more effectively, or perhaps to contact a number of new leads. These experiments are important because they represent the moment when the work of coaching is realised as a change in behaviour. Reviewing the success or otherwise of such experiments provides managers with an opportunity to reflect on their readiness to change, to celebrate their success if change has been achieved, and to explore obstacles if it has not.

DISTINGUISHING COACHING AND THERAPY

The emphasis on the personal as well as the practical journey of coaching raises at least one important question: is a coaching relationship different from a therapeutic one – and if so, how? In some respects the relationships are fundamentally different, in others they are very similar. The key differences are that in coaching:

- The organisation is the sponsor, rather than the individual.
- There is potential for three-way meetings with the sponsor and the manager, rather than just meeting with the individual.
- The focus for change is for the benefit of the organisation as well as of the individual.
- There is an explicit contract with a fixed number of sessions, rather than an open-ended approach.
- There is potential use of external data such as 360-degree feedback and psychometric data.
- Other training interventions may be recommended to support development.

Many people would extend this list of distinguishing factors for coaching to include that it should be short-term, directive and solution-focused. But although this may sound appealing to the sponsor who wants quick solutions, in practice the process of change in coaching and therapy are more similar. Both require an engagement with the personal and the practical. Managers can only communicate with authentic energy if they are freed-up personally to engage with their convictions. As in therapy, working through emotional blocks can be essential for realising positive and sustainable change. These similarities extend to many of the techniques and boundaries of coaching and therapy.

Thus both coaching and therapy can

- be short-term and long-term
- be directive and non-directive
- focus on the present, the past and the future
- link the personal and the practical
- explore conscious and unconscious issues
- engage with emotions and the rational.

In my experience the discomfort that sponsors may have about a deeper approach to coaching is caused by apprehension that personal issues might be explored that are not relevant to managers' development issues, or that personal insights may not be translated into positive change. The coaching approach presented in this book seeks to show that working more deeply with personal issues is not a luxury. It is an essential part of coaching if managers are to develop more conscious and authentic leadership. Sponsors will support such a depth of personal exploration if it is harnessed to manifestly useful change.

In conclusion, the approach to coaching presented in this book challenges many of the traditional distinctions between coaching and therapy, and demonstrates that therapeutic concepts can be usefully applied within the coaching context. However, the approach also highlights a crucial distinction – that coaching has a dual set of goals, personal and organisational, and in this respect it demands an approach that is fundamentally different from therapy.

Summary

Leadership is the process by which managers throughout an organisation exert influence and by which they seek to meet their personal and organisational challenges. There is a tension between personal and organisational needs that, if sustained, leads to authentic leadership, in which personal convictions and organisational goals are consciously and creatively attuned. Polarisation of this paradox leads to defensive forms of leadership, namely defiant leadership or compliant leadership.

The capacity for managers to demonstrate authentic leadership within their roles is dependent on their awareness of self and others. Leadership coaching is concerned with the development of authentic leadership. The journey of leadership coaching contains two parallel aspects, the personal journey and the practical journey, and it is the linking of these aspects that enables managers to translate personal insights into new and useful behaviours.

The emphasis on the personal journey in leadership coaching suggests that, in some respects, it resembles therapy. However, leadership coaching is distinguished from therapy by its practical engagement with organisational goals as well as those of managers.

ENDNOTE

1 The concept of the capacity to sustain paradox as a basis for creativity and authenticity derives from the work of Donald Winnicott. A psychoanalyst working with children as well as adults, he studied how spontaneity, imagination and the development of healthy relationships could be compromised by an 'impinging' environment (Winnicott, 1971). The role of paradox in coaching is discussed in more detail in Chapter 4. (See also Lee, 1997.)

2

The ACE FIRST model of change

 Nothing endures but change.

Heraclitus (500 BC)

A coach needs a coherent model of individual change. On the conversational journey of leadership coaching a model of change serves as a map for making sense of what is happening in the present and what is desired in the future. Without a model we run the risk of proceeding haphazardly, unable to understand why one intervention leads to useful discoveries, while another leaves us lost. A model of change for leadership coaching, with its emphasis on the personal as well as the practical journey, has to be both accessible and deep – accessible in that it can be readily applied to the practice of coaching; deep in that it can accommodate the psychological complexity of change. The model of individual change presented in this chapter, the ACE FIRST model, is a practical integration that stems from a number of psychotherapeutic approaches.[1]

ACE FIRST PATTERNS

The ACE FIRST model provides an organising framework for coping with the complex array of information that is elicited in coaching. I provide an overview of the model and then discuss the various elements in more detail.

The mnemonic ACE FIRST denotes eight aspects that must be considered in coaching (see Figure 6). The three letters of ACE refer to the primary targets for change, and the five letters of FIRST refer to the context in which change is sought.

These eight aspects provide a comprehensive description of how a person handles specific situations, and show how established patterns of behaviour tend to be sustained.

I will illustrate these patterns by contrasting effective and ineffective ACE FIRST patterns for 'giving presentations'. Consider first a manager who gives effective presentations (see Table 3). The manager's 'Actions' will be to prepare in advance of the presentation, to speak clearly and confidently, and to be responsive to questions. These Actions will be linked to such 'Cognitions' (thoughts and beliefs) as 'I'm good at presentations' and 'The audience will like me.' These thoughts in turn will be linked with such 'Emotions' as excitement and positive self-esteem. The manager's 'Focus' of attention will be on communicating clearly and responding effectively to the audience. The effectiveness of

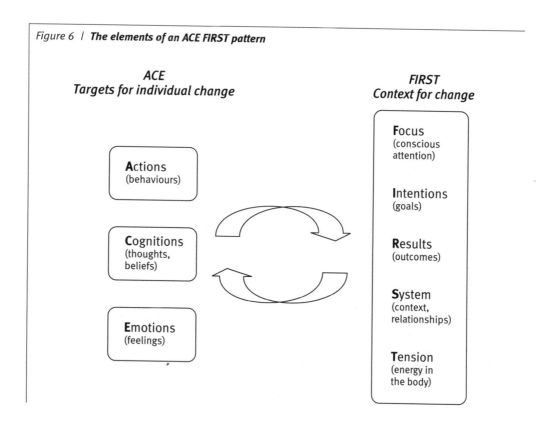

Figure 6 / **The elements of an ACE FIRST pattern**

ACE
Targets for individual change

FIRST
Context for change

Actions
(behaviours)

Cognitions
(thoughts,
beliefs)

Emotions
(feelings)

Focus
(conscious
attention)

Intentions
(goals)

Results
(outcomes)

System
(context,
relationships)

Tension
(energy in
the body)

this ACE FIRST pattern means that there is little gap between intentions and results, so the 'Intention' to communicate effectively fits with the 'Result', which is that the audience is receptive and feedback is positive. From a 'Systemic' point of view, colleagues are supportive of the manager, and the manager may already have a good reputation for giving presentations. From a physical point of view, the manager is likely to feel some 'Tension' in relation to giving a presentation, but this tension is not negatively blocked in the form of mere physical tension, but manifests as positive energy and alertness.

In contrast, consider a manager who has an ineffective ACE FIRST pattern in relation to giving presentations. The manager's 'Actions' are to procrastinate and to prepare at the last minute, to speak too quickly, and to be defensive to questions. These Actions will be linked to such 'Cognitions' as 'I am bad at presentations' and 'They will not like me.' These thoughts in turn will be linked with such 'Emotions' as fear and anxiety. The manager's 'Focus' of attention may be on thinking about past presentations that have gone badly, and on trying to disguise feelings of nervousness. Although the 'Intention' is to communicate effectively, the 'Result' is to appear anxious and ill-prepared, and ultimately to receive mediocre or poor feedback. From a 'Systemic' point of view there is pressure from boss and colleagues to give a good presentation, and there may be a wider pressure to perform because presentations skills are viewed as a key competence within the organisation. Finally the manager may experience 'Tension' in the body as a

Table 3 | An effective ACE FIRST pattern for giving presentations

ACTIONS	FOCUS
(what you say or do)	(your conscious attention)
• *Preparing in advance*	• *Trying to communicate clearly*
• *Checking out who the audience is*	• *Responding effectively to the audience*
• *Looking calm and in control*	**INTENTIONS**
• *Well paced speech*	(your goals)
• *Responding to questions*	• *To put ideas across effectively*
COGNITIONS	**RESULTS**
(what you think)	(the outcomes)
• *'I am good at presentations'*	• *The audience is receptive and engaged*
• *'I will succeed'*	• *There is positive feedback*
• *'The audience will like me'*	**SYSTEM**
• *These ideas are important*	(the context)
EMOTIONS	• *Colleagues are supportive*
(what you feel)	• *The audience expects the presentation to be good, based on reputation*
• *Excitement*	**TENSION**
• *Positive self-esteem*	(energy in the body)
• *Sense of authority*	• *Useful energy that evokes alertness and positivity*
• *Openness*	

consequence of energy blocked, which may manifest as muscular tension, insomnia and headaches (see Table 4).

These illustrations show that there are a range of factors that contribute to how a person behaves within a particular situation, and that these factors are linked together to form relatively stable patterns.

A helpful way of recognising the stability of such patterns is to think about one of your own ACE FIRST patterns. To do this, first of all identify a situation or task that you find difficult, or where you feel you are not as effective as you would like to be. Then take a piece of paper and note your answers to the questions in Table 5. Whatever your chosen situation, you will find that what you feel, think and do in relation to certain contexts is fairly consistent and stable. Furthermore, if you have tried to change this established but ineffective pattern, you may have found it curiously resistant to change.

Table 4 | **An ineffective ACE FIRST pattern for giving presentations**

ACTIONS

(what you say or do)

- *Procrastinating, and then preparing at the last minute*
- *Avoiding practising*
- *Speaking too quickly*
- *Appearing decidedly nervous and fidgety*
- *Responding defensively to questions*

COGNITIONS

(what you think)

- *'I am bad at presentations'*
- *'They will see the gaps in my knowledge'*
- *'I am useless'*
- *'They will not like me'*

EMOTIONS

(what you feel)

- *Fearful*
- *Anxious*
- *Closed*

FOCUS

(your conscious attention)

- *Thinking about past presentations that have gone badly*
- *Noticing anxiety*

INTENTIONS

(your goals)

- *To put ideas across effectively*
- *To survive*

RESULTS

(the outcomes)

- *Anxious and ill-prepared appearance*
- *Feedback is mediocre*

SYSTEM

(the context)

- *Pressure from boss and colleagues to make a good presentation*
- *Organisation views presentation skills as a key competence*

TENSION

(energy in the body)

- *Muscle tension*
- *Insomnia and tiredness*
- *Headaches*

Table 5 | *Constructing your own ACE FIRST pattern*

ACTIONS	FOCUS
• *What did you do?*	• *Where was your focus of attention?*
• *What did you say?*	• *What were you conscious of?*
• *How would others describe what they observed you to be doing?*	• *What might you have been unconscious of?*
• *What were your physical behaviours?*	**INTENTIONS**
	• *What did you wish to achieve?*
COGNITIONS	• *How would you know if you had been successful?*
• *What were your thoughts?*	**RESULTS**
• *What were your underlying attitudes?*	• *What was the result of your behaviour?*
• *What were your beliefs about yourself and others?*	• *To what extent did you achieve your intentions?*
	SYSTEM
EMOTIONS	• *What was the context for your behaviour?*
• *What did you feel?*	• *What external factors or relationships influenced the effectiveness of your behaviour?*
• *To what extent were your feelings hidden?*	**TENSION**
• *To what extent were you aware of your feelings?*	• *How did you feel physically when you showed this behaviour?*
	• *What physical tension did you have?*

THE ACE FIRST MODEL OF CHANGE

The eight factors of ACE FIRST do not represent a full model of change, but rather a framework for describing an individual's experience at a given point in time in relation to a specific context. To use this framework to understand change, we need to consider how ACE FIRST patterns are formed over time, and how they can be shaped to achieve new goals in the future.

ACE FIRST patterns are formed through a combination of a person's history and the predispositions of his or her personality (see Figure 7). These ways of being have been learned through trial and error. Those styles that are effective in achieving a person's goals, within his or her cultural and relational context, are repeated and become assimilated as automatic patterns. Other behaviours, styles and beliefs that are not effective in achieving the person's goals are avoided. These evolving patterns are the strands and fibres that experience weaves into the tapestry of self-identity – into a person's typical styles of talking, thinking, feeling, relating, choosing, understanding, relaxing, celebrating and all the other multitude of ways in which a person comes to live and express his or her individuality.

We can thus think of a person's self-identity as a *repertoire* of ACE FIRST patterns that have become relatively stable. This self-identity is further structured around memories of past experiences and the narratives that are constructed from these memories. *Conscious*

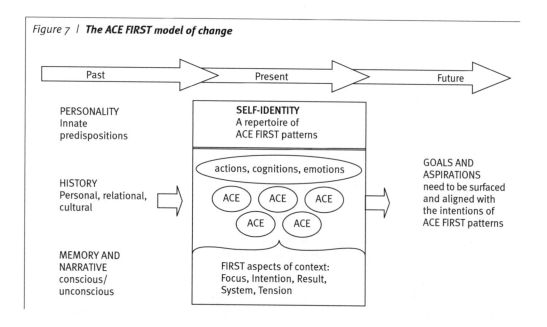

Figure 7 | *The ACE FIRST model of change*

narratives serve as a definition of self – as stories about self-identity that define who a person is, the kinds of things he or she likes or doesn't like, his or her strengths and weaknesses, hopes and desires. The *unconscious* refers to those experiences – behavioural, cognitive and emotional – that lie out of awareness and which are not consciously integrated into self-narratives.

Many unconscious aspects of the way managers operate present no problem because they do not stand in the way of positive change and the achievement of their goals. However, other unconscious factors, often linked with emotionally significant experiences, limit managers' self-narratives, constraining their intentions and their willingness to take the risk associated with new ACE FIRST patterns. If managers can become more aware of these unconscious factors and their impact on performance, they can then challenge the limiting aspects of their self-narratives. Working more consciously, they can confront the emotional blocks that resist change, and so move towards their goals with positive intention.

The purpose of understanding ACE FIRST patterns and how they have been formed is to enable managers to make choices about the achievement of their goals, personal and organisational. Goals and aspirations are examined in terms of the ACE FIRST patterns that are needed to achieve them. In this way the specific intentions of individual ACE FIRST patterns are aligned with the overall goals and aspirations of managers.

USING THE MODEL TO EVOKE CHANGE

Managers bring themselves into coaching with established self-identities – with practised and largely habitual styles that have developed over a lifetime of experiences to achieve their goals. In coaching, aspects of their self-identities become the objects of scrutiny.

Their ACE FIRST patterns are reassessed in terms of their effectiveness. Taking account of the influence of personality, past experiences, conscious and unconscious factors, and the context in which these patterns are being applied, the coach makes interventions that seek to shift emotions, cognitions and actions in ways that will improve performance. If managers' ACE FIRST patterns are effective, the coach reinforces them. If they are ineffective, the coach seeks to understand how to help the manager to change them.

The purpose of the ACE FIRST framework is to encourage awareness on the part of coaches. By holding multiple factors in mind they can more easily consider the nature of the development challenge, and can identify unconscious issues. Whether working as a coach myself or as a supervisor to other coaches, I use ACE FIRST as a mental framework. I visualise the ACE FIRST categories in my mind as I receive information about managers, and I consider which aspect of the framework the information refers to. My listening and questioning can be directed towards sorting things into the ACE FIRST framework, and so towards providing me with a coherent description of the development challenge.

The ACE FIRST model is thus primarily a tool for the coach, providing either a set of mental pigeon-holes for organising information during a coaching session, or a worksheet for recording information after a session. However, the framework can also be used directly with managers – although not necessarily the full ACE FIRST framework. I have found it more useful to use a summary of the framework, which I call an ACE Record (see Table 18 on page 134). (For ease of communication I sometimes refer to 'ACE patterns' in isolation, in which case the associated FIRST elements are implicitly included.)

Having provided an overview of the ACE FIRST model of change I will now track back to describe more fully what is meant by ACE patterns, and by the FIRST elements of context.

ACTIONS, COGNITIONS AND EMOTIONS (ACE PATTERNS)

There are three factors in the model of change presented here that are viewed as the primary targets for individual change – these are actions, cognitions and emotions (ACE). When a person changes or learns, there is a change in one, two and often all three of these components of being.

Actions

Actions refer to what people say and do – their physical gestures, verbal expressions, mannerisms, behaviours, skills and the activities they engage in. In working with actions the coach seeks to elicit a detailed behavioural account of what managers are doing, as if the coach was seeing a video of managers in their work environment. Change in this area is directly linked to the practical goals of coaching, since personal awareness must usually be translated into changes in behaviour if the goals of coaching are to be realised.

Cognitions

Cognitions refer to what people think, how they think, what attitudes and beliefs underpin their thoughts, which thoughts and perceptions they focus attention on, and how they perceive events and make sense of them. By focusing on cognitions the coach seeks to understand how beliefs and patterns of thinking tend to drive behaviour – and, indeed, how they are linked to specific emotions.

Emotions

Emotions correspond to what a person feels. When someone describes an emotion, it is usually by means of a single descriptive word such as 'happy', 'fulfilled', 'relaxed', 'frustrated', 'disappointed', 'worried'. Encouraging managers to notice, name, accept and understand their emotions is a key aspect of leadership coaching, since emotions – and particularly unconscious emotions – are an important potential block to change.

ACE PATTERNS

These primary domains do not exist independently, but are interrelated and tend to form patterns of behaving, thinking and feeling which I refer to as ACE patterns. Someone who is communicating in a positive way (actions) is likely to be thinking positively (cognitions) and is also likely to be feeling happy (emotions). Alternatively, someone who is talking irritably (actions) is likely to be thinking in a critical way (cognitions), and is also likely to be feeling annoyed or angry (emotions). The particular ways in which these domains relate to each other is highly individual and constitute elements of self-identity.

The conscious and unconscious intentions of ACE patterns

ACE patterns are *intentional* – they are intended to achieve certain results. The implicit assumption in saying that ACE patterns are intentional is that all behaviour has a purpose for the individual. Where behaviour helps people to achieve their intended goals it is easy to see the purpose, or conscious intention, of the behaviour. But when people persist with behaviours that do not seem to achieve their goals it is tempting to assume that their behaviour is irrational. A manager withdraws from a discussion, even though he knows he must assert himself to get what he wants. Or a manager demands higher performance standards from others, even though she has demotivated colleagues with her demanding behaviour in the past. In fact these behaviours are entirely rational, but their ineffectiveness results from unconscious emotions and beliefs. The challenge for coaches is to identify unconscious as well as conscious intentions.

Focusing on the effectiveness or otherwise of an ACE pattern facilitates the examination of conscious and unconscious intentions. The effectiveness of an ACE pattern is determined by the gap between its intentions and its results.

- Where intentions coincide with results, the ACE pattern is effective.
- Where there is a significant gap between intentions and results, the ACE pattern is ineffective.

At a conscious level managers may want to achieve certain goals and may know how to achieve those goals – and yet they do not adopt effective ACE patterns. In this case the coach can construe that there are unconscious aspects of ACE patterns that must be explored if change is to be achieved. For this reason it is often useful for coaches to consider the aspects of actions, cognitions and emotions that may be unconscious, as well as those aspects that are conscious. (See the case study about Louise below.)

Working with ACE patterns

The coach, in working with ACE patterns, has a choice about where to focus the need for change. The focus can be on getting a manager to work with new actions, cognitions or emotions, or all three of these areas. In practice, change in one area often ripples through as change in another area. But when change does not readily occur, the coach can shift attention to other components of the ACE pattern in order to get a fuller understanding of why change is resisted.

Coaching focused on developing new skills tends to concentrate on those actions that are effective or ineffective, and seeks to reinforce or teach effective actions. If the manager is able to adopt this learning, then the focus on actions has been sufficient, and there is no need to consider underlying cognitions or emotions. However, if there is resistance to change, or the manager is not able to sustain the change, the coach then explores the cognitions or emotions that may be limiting change. This conscious movement across the domains of ACE patterns, and between conscious and unconscious factors, provides the coach with a structured way of making sense of managers' experiences, and their capacity to change.

CASE STUDY

Louise

Louise – a senior manager receiving leadership coaching – raised concerns about her relationship with a director of the company. The director was fairly new in his role and was reviewing the allocation of certain responsibilities. Louise, although established in her role and well respected, gleaned from a number of sources that the director was not entirely happy with her performance. Certain new projects had either been allocated to other staff or had been absorbed into the director's own remit. Her coach explored her response to this situation in terms of her ACE patterns. First she asked her about her actions: how was she behaving in response to these new circumstances? She said that her response had been to avoid the director. She had taken the opportunity to work from home a couple of days a week and when in the office she worked from a desk where she was unlikely to bump into him. With probing from her coach she realised that in meetings with the director she had become reticent and appeasing, and the coach noted that as she recalled these experiences her face became somewhat frozen. What, her coach asked, did she want to achieve – what was her intention? She said that she needed to understand what was going on with the director, and after discussion with a colleague, had realised that she needed to talk things through with him. However, whenever she considered broaching the subject she felt stuck and would avoid the situation.

Her coach, realising that working only with her actions was not sufficient, chose to explore her cognitions and emotions. Using the trust she had already established in the relationship she elicited information – a fuller picture of Louise's ineffective ACE pattern (see Table 6).

Table 6 | Louise's ineffective ACE pattern

	• *Conscious*	• *Unconscious*
Actions	• *She avoids the director.* • *She is reticent and appeasing in meetings with the director.*	• *She appears frozen and fearful.* • *She crosses her arms.*
Cognitions	• *'I must have done something wrong; I have failed.'* • *'It is safest to withdraw.'*	• *How dare he marginalise my role?'*
Emotions	• *Shame at shortcomings* • *Fear of confrontation/criticism*	• *Anger with director for apparently criticising her behind her back*

Louise thought she must have done something wrong – that she had failed and was perceived as incompetent. These thoughts were linked to the emotion of shame at her shortcomings. A further important thought was that it is safest to withdraw, linked to an underlying fear of confrontation. Furthest out of awareness was her anger with the director for criticising her behind her back, which linked to the thought, 'How dare he marginalise my role, after all my achievements in the past?' These thoughts and feelings, were fuelling her withdrawal from confrontation, and were preventing her from finding a constructive way to tackle the issue.

The shifting of focus across the different domains of Louise's ACE pattern provided the coach with a breadth and depth of information. Understanding the need to probe behind her initial description of the presenting issue, it enabled the coach to surface implicit assumptions and feelings. This raising of awareness was (as we shall see later) an essential step towards helping her not only to change her behaviour, but also to gain insight into some of her core beliefs.

FIRST: THE CONTEXT FOR CHANGE

There are five factors that must be considered as part of the context of change for an ACE pattern. These are:

- the Focus of attention of the manager in relation to ACE patterns
- the Intentions of an ACE pattern
- the Results that an ACE pattern achieves
- the System in which an ACE pattern manifests
- the Tension in the body associated with an ACE pattern.

Each of these aspects is examined below.

Focus of attention

Our focus of attention is usually automatic. But it does not have to be. As human beings we have, at any point in time, a choice over where we focus our attention. Further, where we focus our attention can have significant impact on what we feel, think and do in any particular situation. If we focus on difficulties and problems, certain ACE patterns are likely to be triggered for us, whereas a focus on something fun or humorous is likely to trigger other ACE patterns. Individuals tend to focus on certain aspects of experience in fairly habitual ways, so that their focus of attention becomes narrow, and is itself an integral part of an established ACE pattern. Looking at patterns of behaviour from multiple perspectives is part of facilitating change.

Choice over focus

Awareness that a person's focus of attention is something he or she can choose is as important for coaches as it is for managers. For coaches, this awareness encourages them to think consciously about the options for their focus of attention, and so to think about the implications that may ensue from different choices.

For example, if a coach focuses on a person's weaknesses, the coaching conversations will be quite different from ones where the coach chooses to focus on a person's strengths. Taking another example, if coaches start to feel annoyed during coaching sessions, they may choose to ignore this feeling by focusing away from this apparently irrelevant emotion. Alternatively, they could choose to pay attention to this feeling and to wonder if and how its presence is relevant to what is going on with the manager.

The choices we make about focus, many of which occur automatically, shape the flow of coaching conversations. Bringing our automatic focus of attention into awareness, making conscious our unconscious focus, we learn something about our way of looking. In relation to ACE FIRST patterns this means choosing which pattern to focus on, and which aspects of the ACE FIRST pattern to explore further.

Managers also broaden their focus as part of a coaching experience. In coaching, managers are often invited to shift their focus, to view themselves and their circumstances in a novel way. Whether by providing feedback, asking them to reflect on particular experiences, or to plan for new ways of doing things, coaches encourage managers to envisage themselves differently. For example, from the outset managers are asked to take themselves as their primary focus. This experience can seem strangely unfamiliar for people who spend most of their lives focusing on external opportunities or issues. Similarly, questioning managers about their feelings, as well as possible solutions, shifts the focus to possibly unfamiliar territory. Such invitations to managers to shift from well-worn channels of attention are a central part of evoking change.

Mindfulness

Working with the focus of attention of managers encourages coaches to consider what aspects of ACE FIRST patterns are conscious or unconscious. To change, a person usually has to be aware of what he or she is doing, to be conscious of his or her experiences. The role that awareness or mindfulness plays in change is at the heart of Buddhist practice, by which individuals are taught meditative techniques that enable them to witness their own experiences. Mindfulness by itself can be enough to bring about change, because ways of being are held in place unconsciously.

For example, a manager may habitually react to criticism by withdrawing and feeling depressed. Without being mindful of this pattern it is unlikely to change. But focusing attention on this pattern, the manager can begin to see how it gets triggered and what its consequences are. If the consequences are undesirable, the manager will be motivated to change the pattern.

Memory

However, for change to occur, a person has to *remember* to be mindful. Change usually requires an act of memory. For example, if the manager who withdraws in the face of criticism is aware, at the moment of being criticised, of his potential to repeat a habitual pattern of withdrawal, then he has the opportunity to challenge that pattern. Further experiences of remembering to change in the face of criticism will further reinforce the adoption of alternative behaviours. Thus the ongoing act of remembering to be mindful provides the essential awareness necessary to achieve sustainable behavioural change. Without remembering, mindfully, at the right moment the intention to operate differently, a person will fail to change, unless that change has already become habitual.

In short, at the heart of coaching is the creation of a space in which mindfulness and memory are critical elements, and where the appropriate focus of attention makes the components of an ACE FIRST pattern available for change. Once available, an ACE FIRST pattern can be effectively directed towards achieving its intentions.

Intentions

The first questions we ask in coaching are often: 'What are you looking for – what do you hope to achieve?' Thus we typically start by inquiring about goals and aspirations. These goals will in part be defined by the organisation as part of the contract for coaching. The organisation has an interest in the manager developing in specific ways, and coaching is viewed as a means of achieving those development goals. Such organisational goals must be understood alongside the manager's personal aspirations. Leadership coaching thus has a dual set of goals – organisational and personal – and the aim is to work with the tension between these two sets of goals.

The harnessing of personal talents in ways that are useful for the organisation is, as I have said, the essence of authentic leadership. For example, managers who aspire to senior leadership roles will be more willing to develop their interpersonal skills if they recognise that this is an essential part of the role. The process of bringing to the surface, understanding and developing clarity about managers' aspirations, and their link with organisational goals, is what I describe as 'shaping intentions'.

Shaping intentions

Having an intention implies purpose, the application of will to achieve a goal. That is not to suggest that managers always know what they are looking for, nor know what they are best equipped to achieve in their organisation. Such clarity is itself a part of self-awareness, which is one of the primary goals of leadership coaching. Shaping intentions is concerned with helping managers get clear about what they want, and to explore how this can usefully fit with what the organisation wants. For some managers their declared goals, or those initially highlighted by the organisation, fade in importance as more fundamental purposes are surfaced. In other cases, once initial issues have been addressed, new areas for discussion arise and new intentions are formulated. The process of shaping intentions from high-level aspirations to focused goals occurs in three steps – developing

- hope
- belief
- expectation.

Hope

Hope is concerned with establishing an initial vision, a connection with personal and organisational aspirations that may be short-term, or, as is often the case, may stretch a long way into the future. With hope an intention has a goal to reach for. Without hope there is no starting place for intention, no aim or direction, no search for change. An absence of hope suggests indifference, complacency, or fear, and working to surface the authenticity of hope can be a significant challenge for the coach.

Belief

In the second stage of shaping intentions, the direction of hope connects with the confidence of belief, which is essential to provide the motivation for change. Without the internal courage of belief, when past experience of compromise or disillusionment has fuelled doubt, intention becomes a vain hope, a niggling source of disgruntlement that is best forgotten.

Expectation

In the third step an intention is realised as an ACE FIRST pattern of expectancy, a kind of internal commitment that hopes and beliefs will be achieved in reality. At this stage managers are challenged to convert the unbounded qualities of hope and belief into the tangible and measurable reality of achievement. Without the expectation of change – without an ACE FIRST pattern positively directed towards a desired intention – doubts, fears, or a lack of realism block intentions from being achieved – managers become stuck at the stage of unrealised belief.

Results

In working with change we need a basis for measuring whether change, positive or negative, has occurred – we need to know whether our interventions and the efforts of managers are producing results. In terms of ACE FIRST patterns this means understanding if managers have managed to adapt, such that results are becoming more closely aligned with intentions. As discussed above, implicitly or explicitly understanding whether change has occurred requires feedback on the gap between intention and results. An effective ACE FIRST pattern is one where there is little gap between its intentions and its results. Conversely, an ineffective ACE FIRST pattern is one where there is a significant gap between intentions and results.

In coaching, the primary source of feedback is that obtained directly from managers – from what they say, from what they do, from how they describe their experiences and from their mood. A further source of feedback is from the coach's perception of the manager, and the kinds of feelings and ideas that get evoked in the coach. In addition, there is sometimes feedback from other sources, through observer comments, 360-degree feedback, or data about the achievement of specific performance targets.

Results are useful if they can be compared with intentions. In the examination and gradual fixing of intentions the coach seeks to provide a basis for assessing in subsequent sessions whether useful change has occurred. Without clarity about intention the consideration of results becomes a fluffy process, and the coach runs the risk of collusion, of letting managers off the hook with rationalisations. With intentions held in mind the coach can focus more precisely on the degree of change.

Where results relative to intentions suggest positive change, the coach acknowledges and reinforces the achievement, since recognition is often essential to fuel the intention with further motivational energy. Indeed, reinforcing achievements is often more productive than criticising difficulties. Even where change is only marginal, exploring how to kindle the expectation for further change can be crucial for the subsequent capacity of managers to embrace more significant change. This is particularly the case for managers whose focus for development includes the issues of self-esteem and confidence.

Where results relative to intentions suggest no change, this feedback provides the starting place for a deeper conversation with managers about their intentions, and the aspects of existing ACE FIRST patterns that prevent their intentions from being realised. In this way, whether the assessment of results indicates change or no change, the ongoing process of coaching is guided by feedback about the gaps between intention and results, and further coaching discussions are structured either to reinforce positive change or to understand more about blocked change.

Results v reflection

Although a results focus provides the coaching endeavour with an essential pragmatism, we should be cautious about being overly prescriptive regarding the setting of goals and their measurement. Focusing on results stands in tension with a more open-ended style (see Chapter 4 for a discussion of how the coach creates appropriate conditions for a depth of learning). The danger of a results focus is that it can constrain coaching conversations to an exclusive focus on actions. In order to engage with cognitions and emotions, and in particular to construct a story that entertains the possibility of unconscious issues, coaching conversations have to be reflective and associative. They must permit an emergent and open-ended discussion, to encourage the exploration of thoughts and feelings that are not usually spoken about with other people, and certainly not with colleagues at work. The tension between results and reflection is one that must be sustained by the coach, who makes a judgement about when to encourage reflection and emergence, and when to fix on intentions and results.

System

It is too narrow to conceive of managers as isolated individuals. In working with ACE FIRST patterns we seek to understand how change is constructed, facilitated or inhibited by the context in which it occurs. Family therapists know that there is no point in trying to treat children if they return to dysfunctional families that discourage positive change (Dallos and Draper, 2000). Similarly in coaching we need to think about managers' colleagues and teams, and the wider systems in which they operate (Menzies, 1975; Hirschhorn, 1993). We need to understand how the pressures of those systems and the specific demands of certain relationships can trigger certain ACE FIRST patterns.

For example, a programme of coaching sponsored by two executive directors was targeted at a group of senior managers. The programme was intended to improve staff morale through development of the motivational and interpersonal skills of the senior managers. The managers entered coaching with enthusiasm, having had little development for a number of years, and gained many useful insights about how they could develop their leadership styles. However, their attempts to apply these back in the workplace were repeatedly thwarted by the directors, who refused funding for team-building or social events, who themselves continued to interact in an impersonal way, and who criticised their managers for apparently wasting time on distracting people issues. The coaching initiative for senior managers was destined to fail if the impact of the wider system – the directors' own leadership styles – was not taken into account.

In this particular case, when coaching and team-building for the directors complemented the initiative for managers, it became much more successful. Without addressing the wider system, change would not have been achieved.

Our construction of ACE FIRST patterns and their potential for change can be set within a hierarchy of systemic factors (see Figure 8). ACE FIRST patterns are constructed and realised within a contextual complexity, ranging from specific relationships up to much broader contexts, such as those of the organisation, the culture and the society as a whole.

For example, the senior managers receiving coaching to develop their motivational skills worked in an organisation that had succeeded through recruiting outstanding individuals who could generate substantial revenue. The organisational culture was individualistic and competitive, and managers who failed tended to move on. Employees throughout the

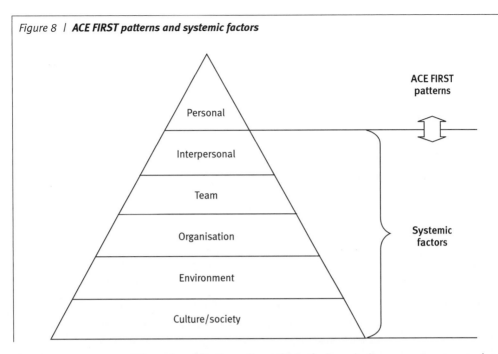

Figure 8 | ACE FIRST patterns and systemic factors

company were conditioned with the view that their priority was to succeed as individuals, even if at the expense of their colleagues. Furthermore, the market environment in their industry at the time of the coaching programme was depressed, and many redundancies were being announced in the newspapers. These systemic factors – the depressed market environment, the individualistic organisational culture and the ambivalence about change evidenced by the directors' own management styles – were the context for coaching.

A coach must take account explicitly of systemic factors, and must discuss their impact with managers. Taking account in this way ensures that the intention to change for managers, which at an individual level is described in terms of developing productive ACE FIRST patterns, is achievable within their working context. Managers have to understand how and what they can do differently, within the realities of their roles, and to plan how those changes can be translated into tangible results for themselves and for their organisations.

Tension

In leadership coaching one would be forgiven for thinking that managers are conceived of as only minds, as if they had no bodies at all. The physical body can be forgotten, even though there is substantial evidence that psychological change and physical change are interlinked. The physical body – and in particular, the place and path of energy and tension in the body – is a further factor to be considered when working with ACE FIRST patterns. A fixing of energy in the body, manifested for example as muscular tension or a shallowness of breath, can be part of the stability of ACE FIRST patterns. In seeking to evoke change, coaches can focus directly on physical tension by encouraging managers to notice how and where they hold tension in the body.

I examine further the value of encouraging movement between tension and relaxation in Chapter 4.

CASE STUDY

Louise, *continued*

Louise's ineffective ACE pattern in relation to the apparent marginalisation of her role by a senior director was summarised earlier in Table 6. The use of the FIRST factors of context can be illustrated by showing how they helped to make sense of Louise's ineffective ACE pattern (see Table 7). I sketch the movement between the ACE pattern and the FIRST factors.

Table 7 | FIRST factors in relation to Louise's ineffective ACE pattern*

Focus	• *She was ruminating on the thought (cognition): 'I must have done something wrong.'*
Intentions	• *At first she had no conscious intention to address the situation.* • *After discussion with a colleague her intention was to talk with the director to understand why he seemed unhappy with her performance.*
Results	• *She was withdrawing and avoiding the director.* • *Despite intending to talk to the director she was stuck, unable to raise the issue.*
System	• *The director was new to his role, was under pressure and wanted to prove himself.* • *The appointment of the director was in response to a downturn in business growth and the departure of a previously influential director. It was a tense time for the organisation.* • *The culture had been informal and friendly, but some people now felt the company needed to be more businesslike.*
Tension	• *Describing the situation Louise appeared closed and withdrawn, with crossed legs and arms, and her voice was a little strained.*

* See Table 6

The ineffective ACE pattern of withdrawal in the face of potential confrontation appeared to be a personal issue that required to be explored in depth. However, it was also clear that the director was under great pressure and might not have seemed approachable. Drawing attention to the systemic factors was helpful for Louise, because she began to see that the director's criticisms might be part of a more generalised anxiety about company performance, and were therefore not necessarily a personal attack.

Encouraged to focus on her intentions and results, Louise identified what would be a desirable outcome for her – a way for her to be valued by the director. Noting her apparent tension as she talked about these issues, the coach suspected that there were emotional factors underlying her inability to confront the manager. Probing to understand the emotional dimension of the ineffective ACE pattern, the coach asked her to describe her experiences of confrontation in the past. Eventually she talked about the relationship between her parents, which had been difficult. Her mother had often been antagonistic with her father, and in response her father had been cool. Her experience of confrontation from an early age was that it led to an awful atmosphere of fear and anger. Louise's response to this situation was automatic and habitual. She would withdraw to her bedroom.

Louise's largely unconscious ACE pattern of withdrawal, learned in an environment of confrontation, was being triggered by the director's criticisms of her behind her back. The link between her past experience and its re-enactment in the present enabled Louise to explore how she could manage her emotions. Moving to the cognitive domain, she identified how her thoughts of failure were limiting her, and she began to focus more on her achievements and to build her sense of self-worth. She also found it useful to notice how her fears were expressed as tension in her muscles and jaw, and she became more aware that she was not only fearful but also angry. She realised that her anger could be put to the service of her intention, which was to find the edge of assertiveness and self-belief necessary to confront the situation. In conversation with her coach, she moved to the domain of actions and rehearsed how she could prepare for a discussion with the director, how she should choose the right time for such a discussion, and what words and gestures would convey her views effectively.

By shifting the focus of attention between Louise's ineffective ACE pattern and the FIRST factors of context that triggered and reinforced that pattern, her coach enabled her to gain insight about why she had been stuck. These insights led her to shift focus to how she could create an effective ACE pattern. She learned how she could contain her emotions of fear, could reinforce her self-belief by thinking about her successes, and could use assertive language and gestures in her communications.

Summary

The ACE FIRST model of change provides an orienting framework for leadership coaching. The model presented seeks to capture the complexity of individual change within a context, but also to be accessible enough to serve as a practical tool to make sense of the factors that help or hinder the process of change. Patterns of actions, cognitions and emotions, ACE patterns, are the primary targets for individual change. A person's ACE patterns develop from the interaction of personality and of individual experience, and are directed towards achieving a manager's and the organisation's goals. These ACE patterns are explored in terms of FIRST aspects of context – the Focus of intention of the manager, the Intentions, the Results achieved, the System in operation, and the physical Tension with which this context is associated.

Working with ACE FIRST provides a framework for the coach to make sense of a manager's experiences, and a means of deciding how to make useful interventions to facilitate change.

ENDNOTE

1 The model of change draws in particular on cognitive-behavioural approaches, solution-focused therapy, psychodynamic theories of the unconscious and systems thinking drawn from models of group and family therapy.

3

The role of the unconscious

The poets and philosophers before me have discovered the unconscious; I have discovered the scientific method with which the unconscious can be studied.

Sigmund Freud (1856–1939)

A year or so ago I was presenting to a group of human resource managers, trainers and personal development specialists who were undertaking a master's degree in coaching and mentoring. The subject of my presentation was relationship development, and for illustrative purposes I discussed a piece of coaching I was doing. I described the difficult relationship a manager had with his boss, and discussed how I had partly made sense of this difficulty in terms of the manager's early relationships with his parents. He seemed to be relating to his boss as though the boss were his aggressive father.

What struck me was the response of the audience during the discussion session. Although they respected the validity of my approach, they expressed extreme disquiet about the idea that coaching should venture anywhere near a manager's childhood experiences, or should seek to make links between unconscious learning from the past and its reliving in the present. Their training seemed to be teaching them that the proper domain of the business coach is the practical techniques for helping managers perform more effectively – that it is dangerous and inappropriate to trespass towards personal history and the realm of unconscious motivation.

In one respect I can support their sense of caution. It is not appropriate for coaches to delve into deeply personal issues with their clients, stirring up issues that they are not qualified to handle. (I discuss the key competencies for coaches in Chapter 9.) However, to rule out such depth of personal exploration per se, to exclude it as irrelevant, is to limit the potential value of coaching. Leadership coaching is concerned with opening up managers to possibilities in themselves that they did not even know about. Further, it is about enabling those managers to lead in such a way that they themselves can open up such possibilities in others. This opening up to possibilities requires a challenge to limiting mindsets and habitual defences. These limiting aspects are part of a person's individual history and are often lost to awareness.

If coaching is to release the vitality of authenticity, it must engage with personal history and the unconscious.

In this chapter I focus on the role of the unconscious in leadership coaching. I examine the psychoanalytic perspective of unconscious processes and the importance of these ideas for making sense of the impact of early experience on leadership style. Finally, I consider the role of 'making links' in enabling managers to be more conscious.

THE UNCONSCIOUS

The unconscious is the fundamental concept within Freud's theory of psychoanalysis (Freud, 1915, 1922; Ellenberger, 1970), and this key concept lies at the heart of all subsequent developments of psychoanalytic theory. He pictured the human psyche as an iceberg, for which there is substantially more below the water than above. The parts of the iceberg that are under water represent the unconscious emotions that underpin much of human behaviour. Making emotions unconscious is a method for dealing with mental conflict arising from tension between different parts of the self, or between internal representations of the self and others.

For example, in the face of being rejected for a job we may behave as if – and believe that – we did not really want the job in the first place. We rationalise away the feelings associated with rejection, rather like Aesop's fox declaring that the grapes are probably sour. Like all adults, we have internalised social expectations about how we are supposed to behave with others. We do not wish to show that we feel hurt, depressed, ashamed or angry – and certainly do not want to express aggressive impulses. Putting these feelings into the unconscious is a way of dealing with such conflictual feelings.

Psychological defence mechanisms

Various psychological defence mechanisms are used to avoid such mental conflict, and these vary from being almost completely conscious to being totally unconscious. The more conscious defence mechanisms include *denial, intellectualisation* and *rationalisation*. The more unconscious defence mechanisms include *repression, projection* and *splitting*. (Repression and projection are discussed further below. A common example of splitting occurs when a manager idealises one colleague and scapegoats another.)

These psychological defence mechanisms serve a purpose in that they enable people to cope with their circumstances without being overwhelmed by painful emotions. However, there are two problems with them.

First, once certain patterns of defences have been established, often early in childhood, they tend to be applied in new situations, even if they are no longer serving a useful function.

Second, the consequence of these defences is a distortion in a person's behaviour,[1] which is often damaging both for the individual and for others. Consider a person – a man, say – who amongst his array of experiences has been strongly affected by a strict upbringing. Let us imagine that this man has responded to his strict environment by accommodating readily to the needs of others, and by hiding his true feelings. As an adult working with colleagues, he now applies his unconscious defence of hiding his true feelings, particularly if he feels angry or frustrated. In cognitive terms he may have developed deeply ingrained beliefs, such as 'I must not show any negative feelings.' There are a number of likely consequences of this unconscious defence and its associated beliefs. Colleagues may take advantage of this man's tendency to accommodate, so the man may work harder than others without receiving full recognition for his contribution. The man may maintain emotional distance from others, which prevents him from forming mutually trusting relationships. From a career point of view he may be perceived as insufficiently confident to take on a leadership role.

Whatever the specific distortions in behaviour, the complex array of psychological accommodations that any person makes to his or her past circumstances are unconsciously played out in the present, limiting the conscious choices about the most effective way to behave.

Of central importance to any endeavour to evoke change in others is the fact that unconscious defences, once established, are powerfully stable. Even if a person knows that he or she is adopting behaviour that is unproductive, he or she may be powerless to change it while the emotions that are being defended against remain unconscious. For example, managers who operate with a command-and-control style may know that they are failing to empower others. However, despite training in motivating others, they will continue to be unduly demanding so long as they have not acknowledged, for example, an unconscious fear of failure, or perhaps an unconscious anger with receiving demands from others earlier in their lives. On the other hand, if managers can become conscious of the influences that have shaped their unconscious patterns, and can acknowledge the feelings of conflict that underpin their defences, they can be freed up to make more conscious choices.

KEY UNCONSCIOUS PROCESSES

Freud continued to develop and refine his ideas throughout his life, and others have subsequently developed them still further into an extraordinarily subtle and sophisticated understanding of human relationships (Greenberg and Mitchell, 1983; Pine, 1990). This is not the place to explore the full breadth and richness of these developments. Rather, I must draw attention to the key aspects of psychodynamic thinking that are most relevant to the work of leadership coaching.

I highlight five key unconscious processes:

- repression
- projection
- identification
- transference
- countertransference.

It is worth noting that many of these concepts have, over the years, been the source of considerable debate and controversy, and in particular they have been criticised for being unscientific and unproven (Szaz, 1962; Cioffi, 1970; Medawar, 1975). This debate has spawned a wealth of useful research, which has now substantiated many of the fundamental psychodynamic concepts. In particular it has proved beyond doubt the existence of the unconscious (Power, 2000; Weiskrantz, 1997; Kagan, 1994), and has demonstrated the operation of key unconscious processes, such as repression (Brewin *et al*, 2000; Power, 1997) and transference (Chen and Anderson, 1999; Glassman and Anderson, 1999; Hinkley *et al*, 1996).

Repression

Repression is one of the most powerful psychological defence mechanisms, which operates to remove threatening feelings from consciousness. Repression may begin as a conscious desire to forget, but such conscious avoidance can become automatic and operate outside awareness. Consequently, there is an unconscious resistance to bringing emotionally-laden memories back into consciousness. This is one of the challenges of coaching, since it is the bringing to the surface of the whole complexity of feelings associated with earlier situations in a person's life that can enable him or her to embrace change with a renewed sense of possibility.

For example, a manager who was shy as a child recalled, among many memories, one of being laughed at by others, both at school and at home. The conflicting emotions of shame, anger and a longing for approval, meant that these memories had been banished from consciousness by repression. In coaching, the manager began to recall these memories when exploring the disproportionate levels of anxiety that he experienced in relation to giving presentations. This led to a fruitful discussion of the different situations in which the manager felt most anxious or most relaxed, and helped him to plan for presentations, less constrained by unconscious anxiety.

Projection

Projection is a method for externalising internal conflicts by unconsciously attributing one's own feelings or aspects of oneself to another person. A familiar version of projection occurs when a person complains about a failing in another when the failing is actually his or her own.

For example, a manager – a woman, say – may extol the virtue of keeping a low profile and getting on with the job, and complain about a colleague who grabs the limelight. Her conscious statements hide her own desire to be the centre of attention. The projection of the desire to grab the limelight onto the colleague may be a way of dealing with painful feelings of inadequacy or envy, perhaps because the manager is not as competent as her colleague, or because she does not have the extrovert charisma necessary to hold the attention of others.

Identification

Identification refers to the process of relating to another person, circumstance or idea on the basis of a perceived similarity to oneself. This can be a conscious process of recognising similarities, and as such can be a useful basis for feelings of empathy.

For example, someone who has lost a job will readily identify with another person who has lost his or her job. The identification with the experience provides the basis for a mutual understanding of the emotions involved. Identification is also a commonplace experience when we hear a story and identify with the hero or heroine.

However, unconscious identification can be more problematic when a person takes on undesirable attributes or feelings and behaves as if they were his or her own. For example, a person can become unconsciously identified with the role of the troublemaker, or the role of the joker. The expectations of – and indeed projections from – others are identified with, and the person may adopt behaviours that limit his or her effectiveness. Similarly, a person may listen calmly to the angry complaints of a colleague about a boss, and then as a result of unconscious identification with the anger, subsequently get angry with the boss too. (The unconscious taking on of other people's projections is the result of a complex process called projective identification, which I examine in relation to countertransference.)

Transference

Transference refers to the unconscious re-enactment of the past in the present. This re-enactment can occur in relation to positive or conflictual emotional experiences, and involves projection and identification.

Where there is *transference as projection*, a person unconsciously transfers and projects onto a person in the present, earlier experiences of a similar person or context in the past. For example, a manager – who had been supported to take on a leadership role by her boss, but had failed in the role, subsequently refused to accept the support of her new boss in extending the responsibilities of her job. Unconsciously the manager blamed her former boss for not supporting her sufficiently in the leadership role, and for exposing her to painful feelings of failure and incompetence. Unconsciously transferring these experiences into the present, she projected her former boss's failings onto her current boss, and consequently refused to expand her new job role.

Where there is *transference as identification*, a person unconsciously identifies with a person in the past, and transfers his or her perception of that behaviour into a similar situation in the present. A simple illustration of this occurs when children adopt the behaviour of a parent in relation to a brother or sister, perhaps by telling the sibling off in the way that they themselves had been told off by a parent. In fact the transference contains both identification and projection – identification with the reprimanding parent, and projection of the child-self onto the sibling. In organisations this process occurs, for example, when managers unconsciously disempower others in order to avoid earlier experiences of being disempowered themselves. There is transference of their earlier experience, but an inversion of roles.

Transference within a coaching relationship corresponds to the unconscious re-enactment of past experiences in relation to the coach. Working with the here-and-now transference can provide the coach with invaluable information about how a manager unconsciously relates to others. The use of the here-and-now transference is examined further in Chapter 5 as part of assessing unconscious factors.

Countertransference

Countertransference refers to the feelings, bodily sensations, thoughts and behaviours that are evoked in a person by someone else. Thus in a coaching session the coach may experience powerful feelings in relation to a manager. The idea that the coach can use these reactions as a valuable source of information derives from the idea that countertransference is the result of unconscious communication (Bion, 1962), and that making sense of the countertransference is a way of making sense of the manager's unconscious experience.

For example, a coach experienced a manager as poised and self-contained, and felt as if there was little she could offer the manager. She felt useless, even though she was a very experienced coach and was used to working with a wide range of managers. In discussion with me we examined the countertransference of 'feeling useless' and looked for what it might suggest about the manager's unconscious experience. In the light of this coach's genuine confidence in her abilities, we postulated that these feelings really did belong to the manager, but they had been unconsciously projected into the coach. The manager, by being cool and self-sufficient, disguised her own sense of 'feeling useless' by evoking those feelings in others. Armed with the hypothesis that the manager actually felt very vulnerable underneath her façade, the coach was able to approach the work with renewed sensitivity, and ultimately engaged the manager in a useful acknowledgement of her areas of vulnerability.

The process underpinning countertransference is *projective identification*, which is an extension of projection. In this case there is not only an unconscious attribution of an aspect of the self to another person, but also interpersonal pressure on the person to identify with, or adopt, behaviours that are consistent with the aspect that is projected (Klein, 1988; Ogden, 1986; Hinshelwood, 1991). In the example, the manager's aloof behaviour put unconscious pressure on the coach to identify with the projection of 'feeling useless'.

Even though it is usually not appropriate to refer directly to countertransference feelings in coaching conversations, the private examination of these feelings by the coach can provide invaluable insight into the manager's unconscious experience. Working with such phenomena carries a danger, however, in that coaches can mistakenly attribute feelings to the manager that actually belong to their own unconscious issues. I discuss the distinction between *countertransference as intrusion* and *countertransference as indicator* in Chapter 5.

Unconscious processes and the capacity to think

The importance of unconscious processes is that they exert an impact on a person's capacity to think (Bion, 1970), and therefore on his or her behaviour and performance. Conscious thought and reflection occurs within a mental space that can contain conflicting feelings. For example, we may feel a duty to be supportive of others and at the same time be irritated with their apparent dependency. Furthermore, we may feel resentful about the level of support that we have provided or received in the past, and these experiences will influence our beliefs and expectations in this area. If we have sufficient mental equilibrium, we can sustain a conscious space in order to think about these divergent beliefs and feelings.

Containing conflicting feelings allows them to be thought about, and ultimately transformed, and such conscious thought is the basis for making sound judgements. Through mental equilibrium, consciousness and thinking, we can make choices about the ways in which our authenticity can be most productively expressed.

However, if formative experiences have been subjected to unconscious defence, then our capacity for thinking is closed down. Rather than containing conflicting feelings we process them unconsciously, such as by splitting them into good and bad, by projecting the unwanted bad aspects onto others, and by repressing them deep into the unconscious. The consequence of these unconscious processes is that we cannot make considered choices about the most useful way to behave. Our actions and reactions are distorted by our unconscious need to remain unaware of painful feelings. Our behaviour carries the mark of defensiveness, often resulting in a polarisation either towards defiantly following one's own needs regardless of others, or compliantly fitting in with the needs of others. In the example above about providing support for others, a defiant defensiveness may lead to an angry dismissal of those who need support, whereas a compliant defensiveness may lead to an excessively sympathetic attitude.

Having outlined key concepts for understanding the dynamic unconscious, I now make a link between the impact of early experience on unconscious defences and the typical kinds of leadership behaviour that managers adopt.

EARLY EXPERIENCE AND LEADERSHIP

Although there are occurrences throughout life that may be subjected to unconscious defence (ie any emotionally charged experience that is pushed out of awareness), the most powerful formative experiences are usually those from childhood in relation to parents. The specific nature of those early experiences, in conjunction with the predispositions of the individual, will determine the degree to which unconscious defence mechanisms are employed.

I investigate different kinds of early experience by examining a particular aspect of psychoanalytic theory called attachment theory,[2] and show how three specific attachment patterns can be directly related to the three primary leadership styles, authentic leadership, defiant leadership and compliant leadership. The linking of such patterns of early experience to specific leadership styles provides a basis for speculating about the typical unconscious issues that underpin these characteristic styles of leadership.

Attachment patterns

Based on extensive research with children and adults, attachment theory has demonstrated the importance of early relationships (or attachments) with parents on psychological development (Bowlby, 1988). If children experience responsiveness from parents – parents who are available, ready to respond when called upon to encourage or assist, but who do not intrude – they develop a 'secure base'. They have an internal sense of confidence that allows them, as children and as adults, to venture into the world, to show curiosity and openness to new experiences, and to form trusting and rewarding relationships.

However, if the early parenting experience is less reliable, attachments and emotional development are less secure. In addition to the secure form of attachment, two primary forms of insecure attachment have been identified (Ainsworth, 1982). *Avoidant attachment* occurs where parenting is experienced as unresponsive or rejecting. *Ambivalent attachment* occurs where parenting is experienced as inconsistent, sometimes ignoring and sometimes intrusive.

I will use these primary types of early parenting experience – the experience of responsiveness (secure attachment), rejection (avoidant attachment) and inconsistency (ambivalent attachment) – to illustrate how a person's ACE patterns (actions, cognitions,

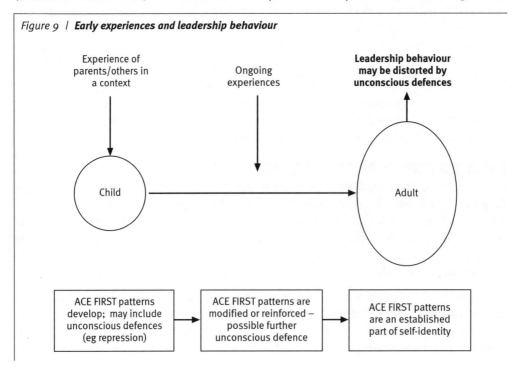

Figure 9 | *Early experiences and leadership behaviour*

emotions) are formed over time. (For simplicity I will not describe the full ACE FIRST pattern.) In particular I will explore how early experience shapes the unconscious factors that underlie adult behaviour, and more specifically, leadership behaviour (see Figure 9).

An early experience of responsiveness

Imagine a young boy growing up in his family. He has particular early experiences resulting from the interaction of his personality, the personality and parenting styles of those around him, and the particular context in which he finds himself. For example, he might play with a toy car. If his mother is responsive, she reacts in an encouraging way, nurturing his experiments and ideas, and delighting in his achievements. The child may move away and play by himself for a while, but then returns to his mother, once again looking for a response. If she is again responsive, encouraging or assisting him according to his needs, then he begins to make sense of the relationship between his actions and the response it evokes – he begins to form a working model or ACE pattern in relation to this context. His actions may be smiling, laughing and trying out different movements with the car. His cognitive conclusions, although implicit and not expressed in language, may be that showing curiosity and spontaneity is good. His accompanying emotion is likely to be happiness.

The child's ACE pattern, which at this stage is only provisional, becomes one of the building blocks of his experience. When he is later with his father, he once again looks for responsiveness. Perhaps he tries an implicit experiment, performing a similar manoeuvre with his toy car and looking to see what response it evokes. Depending on how his father responds, the child's provisional ACE pattern will be reinforced or modified, and will influence his approach and expectations in further situations, whether with his mother, with his father, or with other people in other contexts. Over time, and honed by multiple experiences and interactions which are broadly responsive, his ACE pattern becomes increasingly stable, a reliable way of being in relation to himself and others. Based on experiences of achievement, and reinforcement by others, the child will have an ACE pattern of security and optimism, which may be further reinforced as he grows up and becomes an adult.

Table 8 | Authentic ACE pattern in response to responsiveness

	Conscious	*Unconscious*
Actions	• *Takes effective actions* • *Is assertive and motivational with others*	• *Makes thoughtful gestures to others* • *Displays open expression and posture*
Cognitions	• *Expects and notices recognition of achievements* • *'I can succeed in getting what I want'*	• *Has deep sense of self-belief* • *Retains values of mutual respect*
Emotions	• *Happy* • *Open*	• *Personal optimism* • *Concern for others*

If as a manager in an organisation he is presented with certain leadership challenges, we can imagine that he may apply his ACE pattern of security and optimism, expecting himself to rise to the challenge and to succeed (see Table 8). His positive expectation (cognition), linked to optimistic feelings and constructive actions, is likely to achieve his desired result and to bring positive recognition, thereby further reinforcing his ACE pattern of optimism.

This is an authentic ACE pattern to the extent that it is primarily conscious. There was no need for the manager, as a child, to resort routinely to unconscious repression, because his experiences did not evoke repetitive or overwhelmingly conflictual emotions. Even where there were conflictual experiences, the child will have learned to think about them consciously, perhaps in conversation with a parent, and so will have learned to contain mental conflict and to come to a conscious resolution. The ACE pattern is thus not strongly shaped by unconscious defences, and those aspects that are unconscious are not conflictual or problematic, but simply subject to ordinary forgetting. Consequently, this manager has a capacity to think about how to approach his challenges relatively undistracted by unconscious issues, and so he demonstrates authentic leadership.

So for example, if colleagues offer new ideas, he is encouraging, empowering them to take initiative. If the manager wishes to put forward his own ideas, he presents them with confidence. If he needs to win over dissenters, he cultivates his relationships and looks for mutual interests. If he has setbacks, he responds with determination. If he succeeds, he looks for new challenges. It is the consciousness of such a manager that enables him to be authentic and effective.

An early experience of rejection

In contrast, consider a boy who, amongst other experiences, received disapproval and rejection. For example, on playing with his toy car his mother may frown and tell him to be careful and not to scratch the table. She may take the car away from him angrily, and tell him he is a nuisance. On another occasion he may once again experience his mother's disapproval at his behaviour. If subsequent similar activities evoke similar responses from her, he will begin to form an ACE pattern that is quite different from that of the encouraged child. The disapproval will lead to a fear that he is going to get things wrong, and that he will be rejected.

For the child, the experience of being incapable and unwanted, based on his mother's apparent rejection, is psychologically overwhelming. Since he cannot rely on his mother to nurture his developing sense of emotional security, he needs to find his own way of coping. He needs to get rid of his fears of failure and rejection, and this he does through the unconscious process of repression. His unconscious emotions of fear of failure and rejection are linked to unconscious beliefs that he is neither likable nor competent. The only evidence for these may be seen in certain unconscious actions, perhaps in his eyes, his movements, or his voice, which suggest a need for approval and support.

However, the conscious aspects of the ACE pattern heavily disguise this unconscious agenda. In response to rejection the child learns to appear totally in control and self-sufficient. He demonstrates that he has no need of others, and strives in a driven way to

Table 9 | Defiant ACE pattern in response to rejection

	Conscious	Unconscious
Actions	• Controlling, directive, autocratic • Critical or dismissive	• Looking for approval/ recognition • Looking for support/ intimacy
Cognitions	• 'I must take control to make sure things work' • 'Others cannot be trusted'	• 'I am not competent' • 'I am not likeable' • 'I am not loveable'
Emotions	• Driven • Irritability, anger	• Fear of failure • Fear of rejection • Longing for intimacy

ensure that everything he does is perfect. The cognitions underlying these actions reflect his belief that he must be in control, as well as that others cannot be trusted. At an emotional level he feels driven and irritable.

This complex ACE pattern, reinforced through experience, is carried into adulthood and can be seen most clearly in the manager who adopts a defiant leadership style (see Table 9). Presented with a leadership challenge, he tends to be controlling and autocratic. Unconsciously he transfers his early experience into the present, and adopts the same strategies that he has learned since childhood. He achieves his results through fierce determination and a belief that he can only really trust himself. In terms of his colleagues, he may go through the motions of collaboration, but he is not experienced at genuinely valuing others. When colleagues present new ideas, he is dismissive. When he presents his own ideas, he is overbearing. In the face of dissenters he is a bully. When he has setbacks, he blames others. When he succeeds, he attributes success primarily to himself. It is the unconscious power of his early attachments that sustain such a manager's bias towards defiant leadership.

An early experience of inconsistency

The third typical and distinctive ACE pattern develops from a child's experience of inconsistent parenting. Inconsistency is a result of the parent being experienced as sometimes intrusive and overly involved with his play, or perhaps as overly anxious about his welfare, and then at other times as remote and preoccupied. Unlike the responsive parent, the inconsistent parent is all-or-nothing, and fails to find the happy medium. Consequently, the child adopts an ACE pattern designed to cope with this inconsistent style of relationship.

The emotions that are evoked by inconsistency are partly fear, based on a sense of emotional abandonment when his parent is preoccupied, or frustration and anger when his parent is intrusive and suffocating. However, the child learns that he cannot express these feelings. Experience shows they will not be transformed by this parent's responsiveness, but will evoke either intrusive concern or preoccupied distraction.

Table 10 | *Compliant ACE pattern in response to inconsistency*

	Conscious	**Unconscious**
Actions	• *Collaborative, concerned, appeasing* • *Working and searching for recognition*	• *Appears withdrawn and lost* • *Occasional outbursts of anger*
Cognitions	• *'I must keep the peace'* • *'I will succeed if I follow the rules'*	• *'I am not significant or worthy of attention'* • *'I am furious'* • *'I want to be understood'*
Emotions	• *Anxiety about getting it wrong* • *Fear of upsetting others*	• *Fear of abandonment* • *Frustration, anger* • *Longing for safe autonomy*

Seeking acknowledgement of his fear and frustration, but greeted with inconsistency, leads to increased fear and frustration, which represents a threat to his developing sense of emotional security. To cope psychologically, he unconsciously represses these emotions and the corresponding actions and cognitions within the ACE pattern. Consciously, he copes with inconsistency by being co-operative and seeking approval, and these actions are linked to an anxiety about getting things wrong or a fear of upsetting others.

Carried into adulthood, this ACE pattern can be seen most clearly in the manager who adopts a compliant leadership style (see Table 10). Presented with a leadership challenge, he unconsciously transfers his early experiences into the present and applies that learning. He tends to be collaborative, anxious to avoid disagreement, and vigilant for reassurance and recognition. As far as possible he follows the organisational rules, which he takes to be the safest basis for asserting his authority within his role. When colleagues present new ideas, he does not push them to make them better. When he presents his ideas, he is tentative. In the face of dissenters he tends to back down. When there are setbacks, he blames himself. When he succeeds, he is unduly modest. It is the unconscious power of his early attachments that sustain such a manager's bias towards compliant leadership.

IMPLICATIONS FOR CHANGE

In practice, managers' early experiences do not fall neatly into one of the categories described above. Although managers may show a bias towards one style, they usually demonstrate some flexibility of style according to the specific context in which they are working. In coaching the aim is to understand how specific contexts tend to evoke enabling or limiting ACE patterns, so that managers can make conscious choices that help them to achieve their personal and organisational goals. Where they are demonstrating authentic leadership, the components of their ACE patterns are more available to consciousness, and they will be able to explore new possibilities and try out new behaviours less dogged by the obstacle of unconscious resistance. However, the coaching challenge is more complex when considering those areas where the manager demonstrates either defiant or compliant leadership.

The limits of skill-based coaching

Attempts to coach managers to develop more authentic leadership styles will fail, or only scratch the surface, if they do not take account of the unconscious aspects of defiant or compliant ACE patterns. For example, the manager demonstrating defiant leadership may agree to practise listening, questioning and other collaborative skills with a coach who works at the conscious level. However, the manager's unconscious fears of failure and rejection (see Table 9), while unacknowledged, will ensure that he or she does not adopt these behaviours in day-to-day work. Similarly the manager demonstrating compliant leadership may try to develop assertiveness and an ability to manage conflict. However, unconscious fears of abandonment, and denial of anger (see Table 10), while unacknowledged, will ensure that his or her capacity to change remains substantially limited.

In practice, unconscious factors always have some impact on the performance of managers, and in contrast to a skill-based piece of coaching, leadership coaching provides a space for these factors to be examined. In order to work with the unconscious, the coach needs to create specific conditions within the coaching relationship, and to attend to various sources of information, notably the transference and countertransference, as well as clues and inconsistencies in what the manager does and says.

I describe such aspects in more detail in subsequent chapters. I end this chapter by considering the primary tool for making unconscious issues conscious – that is, the process of making links.

MAKING LINKS

A lack of awareness implies that different domains of experience are disconnected. With the focus of attention narrowed and fixed, like the blinkers on a racehorse, there is only one way to go. In the business setting we often see managers in a frenzy of activity, dashing from one meeting to another, gulping a sandwich at their desks, and making snap decisions. In such an environment the leadership style of managers is necessarily reactive. The mix of experiences that inform and drive their behaviour remains compartmentalised and out of awareness.

One of the primary methods for increasing awareness is to shift the focus of attention across different domains of experience. This breadth and flexibility of focus brings formerly discrete and disconnected chunks of experience into relationship with each other. We make links.[3] Making links about different aspects of oneself and how they connect with different aspects of our environment and circumstances, we develop self-awareness. An explicit intention of the ACE FIRST model of change is that it should encourage awareness of links between the core domains of personal experience and context, and so serve as a framework for self-knowledge and insight.

Patterns and insight

Using awareness to make links invites insight – the realisation that there is a meaningful pattern within a formerly chaotic array of experience. For example, managers who rush from one task to another gain insight when they realise that their behaviour is underpinned by a fear of failure. This insight grows in depth and power when they realise that this fear of failure is linked to a belief that they must be perfect. Their insight takes another leap when they begin to see how the pressure to be perfect was learned in response to pressures from their father, and subsequently from teachers. They gain a further insight when they understand that they can experience their boss as a demanding father, and another when they realise that this association (transference) tends to evoke obedience in them, and to discourage their creativity. A chain of connections and insights becomes the themes of a meaningful personal narrative, a story of self-awareness that gives account of the biases and preferences that can influence future behaviour.

Linking past and present

The personal journey of leadership coaching entails consideration of the past. Without biographical information, coaching is confined to the present and the future – it becomes ahistorical. Some managers would prefer such an approach, saying 'I can't see the point of raking over old coals.' The coach must challenge this view, often based on pragmatism, since links between personal history and present circumstances are often profound and potentially transformative. Where the manager's reluctance to explore personal history appears to be based more on unconscious resistance than expedience, the coach must formulate ideas about the emotions driving resistance, and consider the appropriateness of making explicit links relating to emotions.

Links relating to emotions

Emotion is one of the primary domains of an ACE pattern, and to that extent it is clear that linking emotions with cognitions and actions is a fundamental part of increasing awareness and gaining insight. Understanding managers' conscious emotions within specific ACE patterns can be readily elicited by simply asking 'What are you feeling?' Although managers may need help in articulating experiences that they are unused to expressing, the experiences are nevertheless fairly accessible.

But in the realm of the unconscious, emotions are less accessible. Indeed, certain emotions are themselves the cause of the unconscious. The unconscious comes into existence as a result of the repression of emotional experiences that are conflictual or unacceptable, and in this sense there is always an emotion at the heart of unconscious processes. In classical psychoanalysis, catharsis – the release of emotions – was one of the goals in the treatment of neurosis. Transformation was considered to depend on emotional release.

In leadership coaching there is a need for a degree of emotional awareness, but in my experience it does not have to be achieved in a dramatic way. The linking with emotions is often more oblique. Consider for example the manager I mentioned at the beginning of the chapter, who was unconsciously projecting his aggressive father onto his boss, and was consequently feeling disabled and disempowered in his role. At the outset of coaching he had been resistant to talking about his personal history, and he provided only the sketchiest of accounts. Sensitive to his resistance, I took things very gently, showing mild curiosity about the few personal facts that he did share with me. Gradually, as he gained trust in my capacity to be responsive and to help him to think in useful ways, he provided a fuller biographical account.

My unspoken construction of his unconscious agenda was that he felt angry and retaliatory towards his aggressive dad. He had repressed these feelings because their expression as a child would have evoked further aggression. Consequently, in his transference and projection of aggression, he unconsciously assumed that his boss's irritability could lead to explosive aggression. He could not imagine a lively but constructive debate.

In using this construction I did not seek to explore further the manager's unconscious emotion about his father, which might well have led to a significant emotional release (and which might have been appropriate in psychotherapy). Instead, I made a link between his past and present experience in which the emotional agenda was more implicit. Essentially, I suggested that his experience of his father made him distrust quite normal signs of frustration or confrontation from others, but that in reality his boss might respond constructively to his assertiveness.

The manager was clearly struck by this insight, because he sat quietly for a while. Perhaps this was a silent moment of emotional processing. He seemed to breathe a sigh of relief and then began to discuss how he could test out this idea with his boss. It seemed to me that the unconscious emotional link had been made, however obliquely. My construction of his unconscious agenda had enabled me to intervene in a sensitive way at the right moment, even though I had not sought to share the full details of his unconscious emotions. Consequently, he had begun to look afresh at his relationship with his boss, and to think consciously about his choices for how he could behave.

Creating choice

The great prize of consciousness is choice. Developing self-awareness, making links and gaining insight is the foundation for a person to have options. Without awareness we are controlled, like a robot, by programmed patterns of stimulus and response. Self-awareness provides a way of examining the biases of personality and past experience, and questioning whether those biases are appropriate or useful.

As I have emphasised in this chapter, one of the greatest challenges in leadership coaching is that some of the most powerful biases are unconscious, and if unexamined, will continue to limit a person's choices. By establishing links that address the unconscious agenda, the coach enables managers to expand their array of alternatives. Managers can hold in awareness different options, evaluating them according to their likely outcome, and so use their judgement to make a conscious choice.

Linking does not mean destiny

The past defines our destiny only in as much as we are unconsciously driven to behave in ways that are shaped by it. Linking past and present in coaching is a means for getting managers to undertake changes for themselves that they did not think possible.

For example, a manager's realisation that he has always been bossy since childhood does not mean that he is destined to be a command-and-control manager until the end of his days. Understanding how his bossiness was emotionally learned through interactions with others, in conjunction with the biases of his personality, frees him up to explore new styles of leadership that were hitherto unreachable. The purpose of making a link to the past is thus not to reinforce that connection – quite the opposite. By making a conscious link to the past managers are enabled to challenge or break the unconscious emotional link to the past, and so to loosen the hold that unconscious emotions had on their behaviour and performance.

Summary

The unconscious must be taken into account in leadership coaching because it can exert a powerful influence on the behaviour and performance of managers, and on their capacity to change. In working with the unconscious we can draw on key concepts from psychoanalytic theory, such as repression, projection, identification, transference and countertransference. These provide a basis for identifying and making sense of unconscious motivations. The relevance of these to leadership coaching is that through them, early experiences exert their unconscious impact on managers' behaviours, relationships and performance. Attachment patterns suggest three indicative types of early experience that, through the unconscious shaping of managers' ACE patterns, lead to what I have described as defiant, compliant and authentic leadership. In working with the unconscious the aim is to facilitate self-awareness and insight through making links between different aspects of an ACE pattern in relation to its context (FIRST), between conscious and unconscious factors, between the past and the present, and ultimately between unconscious emotions and business performance. Awareness and insight provide the basis for conscious choice, and more productive working relationships.

ENDNOTES

1 The distortions in behaviour that occur commonly as a result of psychological defence mechanisms correspond in clinical situations to psychological symptoms. Freud's writings cover the impact of these processes on everyday life as well as their impact on the formation of neurosis (Freud, 1914).

2 Although influenced by psychoanalysis, attachment theory is different in two fundamental respects. First, it derives from direct observation of infants who are separated from their mothers, and not from the psychoanalysis of patients. Second, it rejects Freud's concept of instinctual forces of 'libido' and 'aggression' as the sources of internal conflict, focusing rather on emotional issues evoked by disturbances in early relationships, usually with the mother. The relationship between psychoanalysis and attachment theory has been productively developed by a number of commentators, most notably Jeremy Holmes (1996) and Peter Fonagy (1993).

THE ROLE OF THE UNCONSCIOUS

3 The importance of linking as an essential part of the process of thinking and creativity is demonstrated in the work of the psychoanalyst Wilfred Bion (1962). He describes how mental objects are linked to each other – experiences are linked to thoughts, thoughts are linked to words, words are linked to concepts, and so on.

4

Learning

The supreme paradox of thought is the attempt to discover something that thought cannot think.

Søren Kierkegaard (1813–1855)

In this chapter I introduce a five-stage process for leadership coaching, and then explore the first stage in that process – the way in which we create the conditions for *learning* in leadership coaching.

LASER: A COACHING PROCESS

The emphasis within leadership coaching is on the need to develop a depth of understanding of managers as a basis for evoking vitality and authenticity. This depth of understanding must encompass personal history and the unconscious, and relate personal insights to practical changes. The proposed process for coaching provides a frame of reference for moving a manager through the journey of leadership coaching.

The coaching process has five stages:

- Learning
- Assessing
- Story-making
- Enabling
- Reframing.

– the first letters of each forming the acronym LASER. These stages should not be conceived as a linear journey but rather as a flexible framework that indicates the core activities of leadership coaching (see Figure 10).

- *Learning* is concerned with creating and maintaining the conditions necessary for change. The establishment of a contained learning space is essential – it is the foundation for the rest of the coaching journey. This is why, in the figure, the subsequent stages of coaching have been drawn as contained within the learning space.

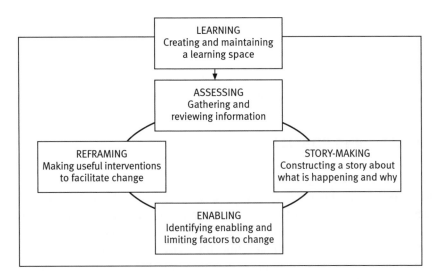

Figure 10 | *LASER: a coaching process*

- *Assessing* is concerned with collecting and reviewing information. This is the stage where the coach encourages self-disclosure, as well as considering other sources of information, such as feedback from colleagues, and the results of psychometric questionnaires.

- *Story-making* is the stage at which the coach makes sense of the development challenge for managers. Hypotheses about change are constructed in terms of a number of possible stories.

- *Enabling* is concerned with distinguishing between those factors that will enable or limit the possibility of change. This stage addresses the fact that there is a difference between having a story about why managers behave as they do, and using these constructions in a useful way to enable change.

- *Reframing* is the stage at which the coach makes interventions that are designed to facilitate change. The term 'reframing' suggests that managers are invited to see an aspect of their experience differently, and as a consequence of this new way of seeing, are able to engage more fully with the practical aspects of change.

An ongoing process

This coaching process does not end with Reframing. The results of interventions at the Reframing stage are reviewed at the Assessing stage, and their success or failure serves to contribute further to the Story-making and Enabling stages. Also, throughout the process the coach is vigilant to the status of the learning space, evidenced by the manager's attitude towards the process of coaching, and the quality of the relationship that is developed between coach and manager. Information about the learning space can provide further information for the Assessing stage, which then becomes part of the overall construction about what is going on for the manager.

The LASER coaching process can be viewed as operating at two levels. At the broadest level it describes the overall journey of leadership coaching, starting with the creation of a learning space and ending with practical actions within the Reframing stage. At a more detailed level it describes the journey that may be travelled several times within a single coaching session, with movement back and forth between different stages, as the coach and manager come towards useful constructions that can facilitate change.

MAKING LEARNING POSSIBLE

Having introduced the overall LASER process for coaching I now turn to the first stage in that process: *learning*. The goal of the coach is to understand how to create the conditions in which a manager is able to learn. I examine the concept of a 'learning space' as the first requirement for enabling managers to make significant personal transitions, and I focus on specific qualities of the relationship between the coach that make such a learning space possible. Then I go on to describe the various practical factors, external and internal to the coaching relationship, that contribute to the creation and maintenance of the learning space.

THE LEARNING SPACE

The learning space is a metaphorical space that exists between the manager and the coach.[1] It can be described as a potential or transitional space in that it opens up the potential for new ways of experiencing self and others – it makes possible transitions from one set of certainties and behaviours to new and more productive ways of conceiving of self and others. As described in Chapter 2, a manager comes into coaching with a developed repertoire of 'ways of being' or ACE FIRST patterns, which as a whole we can think of as constituting self-identity. This self-identity has been formed through experience and personality, and represents aspects of certainty about self and others – it is by definition somewhat resistant to change. In coaching a learning space is created between coach and manager that invites openness to possibilities. It is a space where long-held certainties, conscious and unconscious, can be examined; where fixed patterns of feeling, thinking and doing can be understood in terms of the results they achieve.

The coach's impact on the learning space

I wish to draw attention to three interlinked capabilities of the coach that make possible the learning space. These are the capacity

- for 'not knowing'
- for 'sustaining paradox'
- for 'shifting focus'.

Not knowing

The creation of a learning space depends on a particular quality of the coach that we might describe as 'not knowing'. In stark contrast to the notion of a coach as primarily a wise expert who teaches the manager new skills, the creation of the learning space depends on the coach's capacity for openness, for reflection, for questioning, for wondering, for entertaining possibilities. Not knowing is similar to Keats' definition of 'negative capability', a willingness to stay with uncertainties, without reaching prematurely for fact or reason (Rollins, 1972). The coach sustains a reflective learning space in which solutions and certainties are temporarily put on hold. The grasping for closure is held in tension with a suspension of judgement and a freedom of associations. The coach's capacity for uncertainty implicitly invites managers to question their own certainties. Further, the experience of non-judgement by the coach provides the basis for the establishment of trust — faith that the coach is genuinely motivated to support the interests of the manager.

For example, consider a manager whose self-perception is of being an excellent team player. This certainty about self is built from numerous experiences, and has become a relatively impenetrable self-belief. Any feedback to the contrary is rationalised away. The learning space is created by the coach, who neither agrees nor disagrees with the manager but simply invites the manager to explore experiences of teamworking. Through open questioning the coach teases out memories, reflections, inconsistencies, notes of disquiet, sparks of passion. Without the desire to contradict or challenge the manager, the coach's 'not knowing' sets up a space for thought that was hitherto unavailable.

Sustaining paradox

The coach's 'not knowing' stands in contrast to the manager's certainties of self-identity, and as such the manager and coach present opposite poles of a paradox. It is the sustaining of paradox that creates the learning space. I have already discussed how paradox underpins authentic leadership (see Chapter 1). A manager's personal agendas have to be held in tension with the needs of the organisation, and it is the creative response of the manager to this tension that carries the hallmark of authentic leadership. The relationship between the coach and the manager, with its capacity to sustain paradox, serves as a model for the manager of how authenticity can be evolved and expressed. By avoiding a premature reaching for conclusions, the coach teaches the manager a new way of being that is the basis for personal awareness and insight. The expansion of the manager's awareness about self and context enables new solutions to evolve, and encourages personal conviction in reaching for new goals. Managers create novel ACE FIRST patterns that bring authenticity to their style of leadership.

CASE STUDY

Elizabeth, *continued*

Elizabeth was a highly successful salesperson and was competent at managing her extensive network of external contacts. The operations director supported her strongly, but she had difficult relationships with a number of her colleagues and junior staff. The director felt that she needed 'a few developmental pointers' to address the less positive comments about Elizabeth from colleagues, and encouraged her to receive coaching.

When I met Elizabeth it was clear that she wanted to challenge the notion that she needed coaching. She launched into an account of her achievements and her invaluable contribution to the organisation. She did mention that some colleagues found her tough, but she knew they respected her for getting things done. Then, to my surprise, she proceeded to tell me that she had received coaching twice before. She said that these experiences had been of doubtful value to her, partly because she had been too busy to commit to regular sessions. She was emphasising her self-sufficiency and was also perhaps implying that I could be of little use to her.

I felt powerfully devalued by Elizabeth, and I too questioned whether there was anything useful I could provide her in coaching. Although I could see she was being controlling and defensive, I was struggling to see a way through those defences. What did I need to do to begin to establish a learning space for Elizabeth?

I decided to ask her more about what had happened when she had previously been coached, hoping this might give me some clues about what not to do. She said the previous coaches had emphasised the need for her to commit to regular sessions if the coaching was to be of any use. She acknowledged that this made sense, but also stated that this was impossible for her due to the demands of her role. I was aware of my sense of frustration with Elizabeth. I wanted to say 'Look – take it or leave it. If you want coaching, it's regular sessions. If not – then forget it!'

Perhaps this was exactly what the previous coaches had felt. However, it suddenly occurred to me that this battle for control was exactly what usually happened between Elizabeth and her colleagues, and I was in danger of simply repeating that pattern. In terms of the learning space I realised that I needed to show my capacity to sustain paradox for her, neither judging her nor trying to control her. I found myself saying to her, 'Whatever we do today, I think we should agree that committing to a piece of coaching is not possible. That does not mean that we cannot have one or two ad hoc sessions just to explore some ideas, but we must agree that this is a loose and informal arrangement.'

My response to her controlling style was to show her that I did not need to control her. Furthermore, I showed myself to be open to the possibility that she did not even need coaching. My proposal did seem to defuse her defensiveness and she used the rest of the session to talk a little more openly about her work role. However, I still wondered if she would ever come back for another session.

CASE STUDY continued

In fact, the result of my attempt to create a learning space must have made a difference for Elizabeth. She organised a second session with me. In that session she declared her decision to focus on her personal development using coaching, and that to do that she was determined to commit herself to a series of regular sessions. I was a bit taken aback, and I asked her what had made her change her mind. She said my comments about agreeing not to commit to coaching had made her realise how defensive she was being. I was struck by the complete reversal in her perspective. In the first session she presented herself as totally competent and invulnerable. In this second session she was presenting herself as more open to exploration. It seemed to me that by seeking to create a learning space for her, sustained through paradox, she had managed to take ownership for her need to develop. She had made the first step towards developing authentic leadership.

Shifting focus

Within the reflective frame provided by 'not knowing' and the sustaining of paradox, the coach needs to be able to shift focus, to understand managers' experiences from different viewpoints. This entertaining of multiple perspectives suggests that there is not a single truth about the way in which experiences are understood, but rather that different explanations and stories can evolve from different views; that learning occurs more readily in a multifaceted context of competing realities. (For example, in Chapter 2 I talked about shifting the focus of attention to different elements of an ACE FIRST pattern.)

In the context of the learning space this shifting of focus provides managers with the experience of the coach as both empathising with the learning challenge and standing as an outsider commenting on their challenges. There is a movement between the manager's and the coach's perspective that is carried by their dialogue. The appreciation of the many-faceted nature of the issues contributing to learning and change, where all aspects are open for consideration, sets the tone for the learning space. It invites playfulness and an open-ended attitude to new possibilities.

However, this open-endedness itself must be held in tension with the need to be results-focused. In the real world of business coaching, managers require a sense of engagement with their work challenges, and become justifiably intolerant of an approach that seems indulgently open-ended. In my experience managers are willing to explore issues in great depth, and from many perspectives, if they know that the coach carries a responsibility for helping them to achieve real results. To this end I have found it useful to be aware of shifting focus in the context of a particular dynamic – that is, the dynamic between 'being' and 'doing'.

The dynamic of 'being' and 'doing'

The difference between being and doing provides a useful way for the coach to think practically about the shifting focus of attention. The pull towards being or doing can be

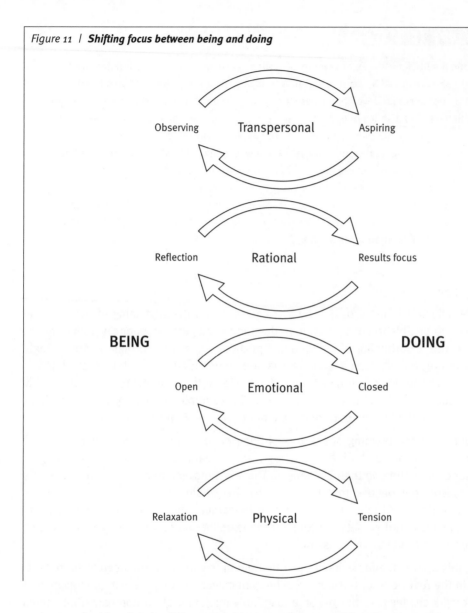

Figure 11 / *Shifting focus between being and doing*

Observing   Transpersonal   Aspiring

Reflection   Rational   Results focus

BEING   **DOING**

Open   Emotional   Closed

Relaxation   Physical   Tension

understood at four levels of the manager's experience – physical, emotional, rational and transpersonal (see Figure 11). The learning space is one in which there can be a fluidity of movement between these aspects of being and doing.

The physical dimension

In Chapter 2 I talked about how physical tension can influence a manager's capacity to change. Physical tension is an indication of stress, and the tightening of muscles and other physiological responses corresponds with a person's need to cope with his or her circumstances. These physiological responses are part of our evolutionary heritage, the reflex for 'fight or flight' triggered by a predator or adversary that enabled our species to survive the dangers of the jungle. Although the work environment may not seem to threaten survival in this way, the constant pressure to produce results, to win sales, to negotiate solutions, to handle conflict, to compete – these create the experience of a present-day jungle, and can evoke the same kinds of physiological responses. Physical tension becomes part of a manager's habitual styles, part of the certainty of self-identity. In examining physical tension, the coach seeks to understand how a person's body can lock him or her into repetitive patterns of being and relating.

Physical tension manifests in a number of ways – tension in the neck, the back, or the stomach; a shallowness or tightness of breath; a clenching of the jaw or fists; a restlessness that shows as a tapping of feet, or fidgeting with a pen. Furthermore, physical tension can have a wider physiological impact – for instance as headaches, migraine, insomnia, stomach ulcers and even heart disease. Although it is not the job of the coach to take the role of a doctor, it is also not appropriate to ignore a person's body.

By wondering about tension and the way in which it is expressed, the coach seeks to provide a basis for movement between tension and relaxation. Encouraging managers to notice tension allows them to consider consciously their relationship with their bodies. In what ways do they look after themselves physically in terms of diet and exercise? How often do they get ill, and in what way is this connected with stress? To what extent is their breathing and posture sustaining tension?

For example, I encouraged one manager to notice how he held his breath as he pondered issues, and that this holding of breath seemed to constrain his thinking. Focusing on breathing more deeply and slowly provided him with a new kind of self-experiencing that helped to open him to the possibility of change. The aim of such focusing is not to move a manager towards relaxation as a static goal, but to create a greater flexibility of movement between tension and relaxation, and so to open the door to new ways of being.

The emotional dimension

In parallel with the bias towards tension in the body is a bias towards being closed to emotions. At work, emotions are usually either ignored or regarded with considerable caution, particularly if those emotions are difficult ones. Many managers talk about the need to 'put on a brave face', or to 'show a stiff upper lip', even though emotions of frustration, disappointment or worry need to be acknowledged. The inappropriateness of emotions at work becomes part of the norms of an organisation.

The need to contain emotions, just like the need for physical tension, is a necessary part of the process of doing. However, the holding of emotions is also a key cause of resistance to change. In coaching, the learning space has to be one in which there is openness to emotions as an important basis for developing self-awareness.

The rational dimension

A manager's work is usually dominated by the need to apply rationality to achieve results. The overall purpose of coaching is usually framed in similar terms: to improve management performance. While the coach must hold the overarching goals of coaching as paramount, the learning space requires a movement between being results-focused and taking a more reflective stance. Reflection implies an ability to stop, to introspect, to examine a wide range of factors and to see what emerges from this exploration.

It is common for managers in coaching to foreclose on the first solution that comes to mind. Where producing a result quickly is the measure of good performance, making quick decisions and taking action is the habitual style. However, it is inevitable that such rapid decision-making can only draw on a person's existing decision-making styles. Whatever biases managers may have, if forced to react quickly they will apply the best-known solution they have to hand. An exclusive results focus invites a repetition of previously-tried behaviour, and as such discourages change. In contrast, the sustaining of a learning space encourages a movement between reflection and a results focus, and permits managers to become more conscious of their options.

The transpersonal dimension

The transpersonal dimension refers to aspects that are beyond the individual, and is concerned with a person's experience of meaning in life, with spiritual possibilities, and with a person's need to reach towards the larger issues that face himself or herself, society and the world. The transpersonal dimension is one that is usually completely ignored by coach and manager alike, as if existential issues have no relevance to business performance. However, it is in a manager's aspirations that we can often find an expression of the transpersonal. Underpinning a person's choice of career, whether in business, education, medicine, law, politics, or technology, is not only a personal desire to achieve particular goals, but also a transpersonal need to contribute in some way – perhaps to be a better parent than one's own parents, to support a family, to contribute to society, to raise the quality of life for others, to provide opportunities for more people, to ensure that justice is achieved, to create a fairer society.

For many managers these aspirations have become remote. In the context of organisational life, with its primary drive for improved performance and promotion, transpersonal aspirations are forgotten, or are narrowly defined in terms of survival. The aspiration has become one of changing in reaction to circumstances, and ensuring organisational survival. Such a survivor mentality tends to maintain the status quo, and as such, blocks the capacity for transformation. Survival implies coping, as opposed to excelling.

In the learning space managers are invited to think afresh about the aspirations that will bring meaning to their lives. That search for deeper aspirations is achieved by a movement towards goal-less observation. Through a non-reactive witnessing of themselves, managers come to know more about what really matters to them in their lives. The observing aspect of the transpersonal dimension operates in tension with the aspiring aspect, where essential values and needs are translated into visions of personal contribution.

CASE STUDY

Greg

Greg undertook leadership coaching as part of his transition to a more senior role within marketing in the pharmaceutical industry. He was committed to the process of coaching, but his style tended to limit his focus to specific business issues. In thinking about the learning space, I considered how he operated at the four levels of 'being and doing'. At a physical level Greg seemed measured. His movements were precise and considered, as if he could not allow himself to be spontaneous. At an emotional level he seemed closed. He did not express feelings, describing only the practical challenges of his role, and commenting objectively on his colleague relationships. It was at the rational level that he seemed most comfortable, expressing himself with logic, showing great reason in evaluating issues, and readily identifying personal development targets. When I asked about his wider sense of contribution, moving the focus to the transpersonal dimension, he offered an uninspiring aspiration of corporate survival, expressed as a desire to help the business to succeed in a competitive environment.

Greg presented a common bias towards 'doing' at each of the four levels. In response, I decided to open up the learning space such that there could be movement back and forth between 'being' and 'doing'. Within the physical domain, it transpired that Greg made little time for exercise and routinely suffered with a stiff neck. We noted his tendency to hunch his shoulders and to wrap his legs around each other, and discussed what these physical gestures might suggest. They seemed to indicate his desire to control anxiety.

Encouraging him to be open to this and other emotions, he allowed our discussions to have a slower pace, with brief periods of silence when he could allow associations to surface. This shift towards being as well as doing helped Greg to explore the transpersonal domain. He began to talk about the aspirations he had had at the beginning of his career. He had considered training as a doctor because he liked the idea of helping others, but had joined the pharmaceutical industry because he was also attracted to business. The important link for him was that a role in the pharmaceutical industry represented a desire to make a difference through healing others. However, he realised that this rather noble goal had been forgotten through his years of success and promotion. Indeed, it was an aspiration that he was embarrassed to discuss with colleagues, who, like him, felt compelled to talk primarily about profitability and market shares. This insight provided a useful focus for the coaching – it indicated how Greg could be enabled to re-experience his excitement for the pharmaceutical industry, and its potential contributions to healthcare.

THE PRACTICAL MANAGEMENT OF THE LEARNING SPACE

So far I have talked about the learning space as underpinning the work of leadership coaching. The learning space is created and sustained by certain capabilities that the coach brings to the relationship, namely 'not knowing', 'sustaining paradox' and an ability for 'shifting focus'. However, these qualities are not sufficient in themselves to ensure that a learning space is sustained. The coach also has to manage a number of other factors that impact on the learning space:

- the organisational sponsorship of coaching
- the boundaries of the coaching relationship
- resistance to coaching.

Managing the sponsor

Leadership coaching is sponsored by the organisation, and so an understanding of an organisation's goals for coaching will have an impact on the learning space. Where the sponsor and the manager are the same person, the context for coaching is simpler because there is no third party. Where the sponsor is a boss or a human resource manager, or the coaching is part of a programme of development for a group of managers, the coach has to pay specific attention to how the sponsor may support or undermine the learning space.

The supportive sponsor

The supportive sponsor is a boss or human resource manager who provides clarity about an organisation's expectations from coaching. The decision to sponsor coaching is taken as part of a wider appreciation of the challenges facing the organisation, and these are connected with the developmental challenges of individual managers. The coach will typically meet with the sponsor, sometimes at the same time as the manager, to discuss development goals, to agree the boundaries of the work, and to plan how the effectiveness of the coaching will be evaluated. This discussion of goals, boundaries and evaluation enables the coach to manage possible tensions between the organisation and managers, and to make such tensions a useful part of the learning space.

The undermining sponsor

The management of the learning space is more problematic when the sponsor has a hidden agenda. In these circumstances the sponsor's actions can undermine the learning space, either making leadership coaching very difficult or destining it to fail. I examine two common types of sponsor that undermine the learning space: the 'sabotaging' sponsor and the 'avoidant' sponsor.

The sabotaging sponsor

Sponsors can appear to support coaching even though their unconscious agenda is more complicated. On the surface, bosses know that they will be assessed on their capacity to develop and support staff, and so feel compelled to encourage development initiatives. However, this can be at odds with a reluctance, conscious or unconscious, to support others, often because bosses themselves feel unsupported in their own development needs, or because they feel threatened in their competence by junior staff. In such circumstances sponsors may sabotage coaching. The sabotage can manifest itself in a number of ways, such as:

- placing unrealistic limits on the number of coaching sessions
- forcing the person to cancel sessions at minimal notice in order to attend business meetings
- failing to provide useful feedback on the person that would facilitate effective coaching
- providing little or no support for the changes that the person has identified from coaching.

Recognising how these factors can undermine the coaching endeavour empowers human resource managers and coaches to explore ways of addressing the potential sabotage. Typically, this means working to gain the commitment of sponsors, providing more support for them, and making explicit what support is needed to make coaching a success. The agenda of sponsors is thus addressed by proactively pointing out how they can inadvertently undermine the process. In some circumstances sponsors can be encouraged to consider their own development and to undergo their own coaching.

The 'avoidant' sponsor

Bosses and human resource departments sometimes sponsor coaching when they are reluctant to confront an issue, perhaps where a bad recruitment decision has been made, when there are sensitivities about discussing underperformance, or where the boss dislikes confrontation and would like to pass the issue on to someone else. In these circumstances it is essential that the coach, possibly in conjunction with a human resource manager, takes time with the sponsor to surface the real issues behind the choice of coaching. The key questions include:

- What are the goals of coaching and to what extent are they achievable within the time and resources available?
- What will be the consequences for the person if the coaching does not achieve the intended goals?
- What ongoing support are the sponsor, and the organisation as a whole, prepared to provide for the individual as he or she seeks to make these changes?
- What has the sponsor already communicated to the individual about the purpose of coaching, and about the way in which a positive change in performance will be measured?

> ### CASE STUDY
>
> **Sarah**
>
> A director took the initiative to recruit Sarah whom he had worked with in the past, and who had 'usefully shaken things up' in a previous role. After a year her performance was poor, she had distant relationships with other members of the team, and there had been a significant complaint from a customer. It was apparent that her abrasive style suited neither the culture of the team nor the expectations of customers. The director, resistant to acknowledging that his recruitment decision had not worked, decided to sponsor coaching for her.
>
> Although the coaching was useful to her, the organisation was not really committed to providing the degree of support that would have been necessary to make significant change. The hidden agenda from the point of view of the director was that, through coaching, she would realise that she should move job or leave the company. His avoidance of stating this, either to her or to the coach, was unconsciously motivated by his sense of shame about his poor recruitment decision, and his guilt about rejecting someone he had formerly encouraged to take the risk of leaving her previous company. Consequently, the coaching took as its goal her assimilation into the department.
>
> Despite improvements in her performance, she was subsequently asked to leave the company – the director had finally been compelled by colleagues to confront the fact that she had not been a suitable recruit. If this had been made explicit at the outset, coaching could more usefully have focused on an examination of alternative career opportunities, inside or outside the company, and could have supported her in making a career transition.

Managing boundaries

The psychological boundaries of the learning space are sustained by the determination of the coach to favour thinking and insight in preference to easy answers. These psychological boundaries are supported by the practical boundaries of coaching. The effective management of these practical boundaries is an important part of the learning space. I consider three practical boundaries:

- the coaching contract
- the role of confidentiality
- the setting for coaching.

The coaching contract

The contract lays down the primary parameters within which coaching will be conducted – the duration, number and length of sessions, the fees for sessions and the policy on cancellation. The explicit nature of these boundaries serves to define the coaching relationship as a particular entity that sits outside the day-to-day activities of business life. Typical aspects of the coaching contract are:

- There must be a statement about the goals of coaching and the way in which the achievement of goals will be evaluated. Although goals often evolve during a series of coaching sessions, fixing useful organisational endpoints for the work is an essential part of managing the expectations of sponsors and managers.

- The duration and number of sessions of coaching can vary considerably. Leadership coaching with a senior manager may be typically 10 to 20 sessions over a 9- to 12-month period. However, the duration of coaching can be shorter or longer than this. At its shortest a manager can achieve substantial personal insight during a single follow-up session to a training programme, as long as the coach or trainer is sensitive to the nuances of the learning space. At the other end of the spectrum, coaching can proceed on an open-ended basis.

- The length of sessions needs to be specified. A typical session is 1½ hours, although this varies according to the availability of the manager. For example, it is common to have one-hour sessions in investment banking, but two- or even three-hour sessions in industries where managers' roles demand frequent travel.

- The commitment to coaching on the part of the sponsor and the manager must be explicit. This is partly signified by the agreement of fees for coaching, but is often particularly highlighted by attitudes towards cancellation. Although it is necessary for the coach to be flexible and realistic about the demands on the time of managers, it is important for coaching to be viewed as a priority to which managers and sponsors are committed. An explicit cancellation policy can help to test commitment to the process. A typical cancellation policy may be to charge the full rate for sessions cancelled with less than 48 hours' notice, and to charge 50 per cent for sessions cancelled with less than five days' notice.

Confidentiality

The issue of confidentiality is typically contained within a written contract, but must also be discussed by the coach with the manager. Clarity about confidentiality is essential for the learning space, since the manager will not self-disclose to an indiscreet coach. It is usual for the detailed content of coaching conversations to be completely confidential, although the manager should be informed that as part of maintaining professional standards, the coach may discuss aspects of his or her work with an external supervisor, who is also bound by the rules of confidentiality. (The role of supervision is discussed in Chapter 9.)

Sometimes it is expected that the manager and/or the coach will provide a summary of the developmental conclusions coming out of coaching work, and in this case the information that will be passed to the sponsor is discussed in advance by the coach and manager. In my experience it can be particularly useful to undertake a three-way discussion between the manager, the sponsor and the coach at the end of the coaching assignment, with the explicit purpose of identifying how the manager will require to be supported in furthering his or her development within the work role.

The setting

The setting refers to the location and the particular environment in which the coaching is to take place. The environment must be comfortable and private, without interruptions from others. Seeing managers outside their offices can often help them let down their managerial façades, and so make better use of the learning space. Furthermore, some managers report that they enjoy the time it takes to travel to and from coaching sessions, since this time provides time for reflection either side of coaching conversations.

However, seeing managers at their place of work also has its advantages, since it provides the coach with first-hand experience of a manager's working environment.

Whichever setting is chosen, the coach must think about its impact on the learning space, and to make changes if necessary. For example, one coach found she was regularly assigned a meeting room with glass walls, adjacent to a large open-plan office. In such an exposed setting it was impossible for her to create a productive learning space.

Managing resistance

Working with resistance is one of the key challenges of leadership coaching, because underlying resistance are often the personal insights that make change possible. Working with resistance is an ongoing part of coaching, and its management can have particular relevance to the learning space. Sensitivity by the coach to the possible causes of resistance can indicate what needs to be addressed to reinforce the learning space.

There are numerous possible signs of resistance, such as cancelling sessions at minimal notice, finding excuses to shorten sessions, being called away during sessions, being overly joky or overly formal, complying too readily or constantly challenging. Resistance can take many forms, and the same piece of behaviour from two managers cannot necessarily be interpreted in the same way. For example, one manager's theoretical bias in a conversation may be part of how they learn best; another's may be a way of resisting a discussion about more significant issues.

In working with resistance the coach must:

- view resistance as a clue to the manager's psychological experience of change, and possible discomfort with the learning space
- formulate hypotheses about what may be the cause of the resistance
- question in a way that tests the hypothesis
- decide if and when it is necessary or useful to comment on resistance in a way that supports the learning space.

CASE STUDY

Hugh

The coach agreed with Hugh, a middle manager, that their first session would last for two hours, giving them time to get to know each other and to plan how to use the coaching relationship going forward. The session began on time but after about 30 minutes Hugh received a call on his mobile phone. After a few moments' conversation he turned to his coach, apologised, and said that he would need to 'pop out for a moment'. The coach was taken off guard and she did not have time to reply before he left. As the time ticked away the coach wondered what crisis had arisen – surely a major crisis could be the only explanation for such an abrupt departure and prolonged absence. Hugh returned after more than 40 minutes, apologised for keeping the coach waiting, and said, 'So what are we going to do in these coaching sessions?'

In Hugh's absence the coach had time to reflect on what might be going on. When interrupted by the telephone call she had been asking him to describe certain aspects of his personal history – what were his key relationships and experiences? She suspected that Hugh's sudden departure, following the telephone call, was an opportunistic escape from the conversation: he was showing resistance. She hypothesised that he felt resistant to talking about his personal history, and decided to test this out when he returned.

Rather than colluding with Hugh's desire to push the focus back onto the coach to talk about 'what we are going to do in these coaching sessions', she chose to ask him about why he had needed to disappear for so long. What had happened? He looked a bit awkward and then admitted that his new electronic diary had been delivered to reception, and that he had had to go and sign for it. Furthermore, he had then taken it to his desk and spent some time loading information from his laptop computer onto the electronic diary.

Hugh's apparent gall astonished the coach. However, she contained her outrage, which he seemed to be intentionally provoking. Instead, she asked him to talk about how he felt about coaching as a space in which he could look at past as well as present experiences, and explore the links between the two.

This change of tack surprised Hugh, undercutting his cheeky arrogance, and he acknowledged that such areas of discussion felt unfamiliar and uncomfortable. His acknowledgement of discomfort gave the coach an opportunity to address his resistance. She noted that at first most managers can feel uncertain about coaching, and that they may find themselves using other business commitments as a way of avoiding this uncertainty – by for example cancelling sessions, or getting distracted in the middle of a session. Hugh laughed at this, and also looked a little relieved.

By forming a hypothesis about the underlying cause of resistance, and then testing that hypothesis through questioning, the coach had managed Hugh's resistance and had begun to create a useful learning space in which productive coaching could begin.

Summary

The learning space is a metaphorical space, arising between the coach and manager, that makes possible the reflection necessary for fundamental personal change. This space is created and sustained by particular capabilities of the coach, namely 'not knowing', 'sustaining paradox' and 'shifting focus'. The shifting of focus occurs, in particular, in relation to the distinctions between being and doing at different levels of the manager's experience. The creation of the learning space by the coach's styles of thinking, is reinforced by certain practical management issues – the management of the sponsor, of boundaries and of potential resistance to change.

ENDNOTE

1 The concept of the learning space is based on the work of Donald Winnicott (1971), who put forward the notion of a potential space as an essential experience necessary for learning and development. In its earliest form in a person's life the potential space exists between a child and its mother, and gives rise to a transitional object, often in the form of a favourite blanket or teddy bear. The psychological significance of this learning space is critical for the child, because the challenge is to learn what aspects of the world are parts of 'me', and what are not parts of 'me'. The child begins with the experience that the world corresponds to my needs and desires, and to that extent the world is an extension of me. But as the child develops psychologically, there is a need to understand that the social world is filled with other people whose agenda is not solely to satisfy the child's own needs (something even some adults have not learned!). The potential space, or learning space, is a stepping stone between these two views of the world – it sustains the paradox that both of these views are true. For the child, the teddy bear is both 'me' and 'not-me'. It is the sustaining of this ambiguity within the learning space that allows the child to make sense of the experience – to create his or her own authentic perspective. In contrast, if the apparent reality of the world is imposed prematurely from outside, then authenticity is hidden behind an unconscious façade of compliance (a 'false self').

5

Assessing

I must begin with a good body of facts . . .

Charles Darwin (1809–1882)

Assessing is the second stage in the LASER coaching process and is concerned with gathering information. Within the boundaries of the learning space, the coach elicits and collects together the manager's multifaceted experiences. Assessing is a distinct stage in the sense that there are periods, particularly at the outset, when the coach's primary focus is on data collection. However, in another sense assessing is interlinked with all other stages of the coaching process.

The initial creation of *the learning space* (first stage) inevitably occurs at a time when the coach is asking questions about the goals for coaching, and so *assessing* takes place from the outset. As the coach begins to receive information, there is a need to make sense of it in order to discern what question to ask next – and this process of making sense involves *story-making* (the third stage). Further assessing activities – questioning, commenting, or being silent – reflect the coach's judgement about what will *enable* (fourth stage) the manager's openness and motivation, and the focus of questions can invite the manager to *reframe* (fifth stage) experiences, seeing them from a new perspective.

Assessing is thus a distinct stage of coaching that is also interwoven with all other stages. In this chapter I outline the aims of assessing, the different sources of information and the types of questions required to elicit useful information. I also consider unconscious resistance to change, and the use of transference and countertransference information for making sense of these unconscious issues.

THE AIMS OF ASSESSING

As I noted in Chapter 1, leadership coaching entails a personal and a practical journey that takes account of emotional factors as well as the skills necessary for improved performance. The aims of assessing reflect these parallel agendas:

- to gather information about the personal and practical experiences of managers as a basis for constructing a story, or stories, about their development challenges

- to invite managers to view present circumstances and challenges as part of a continuum of experience, from the past, through the present, to the future, and to gain a sense of their capacity to shape this journey
- to identify areas for development that encompass individual and organisational needs, and that take account of potential tensions between these needs
- to collect information to fit against the ACE FIRST model of change, identifying aspects of managers' ways of being that are more effective within specific contexts and those that are less effective
- to consider how conscious and unconscious factors may influence the capacity of managers to change
- to identify what managers are motivated to achieve
- to collect information in a way that triggers the resources and strengths of managers to learn and change.

To address these aims, the coach must gather information about a number of domains of managers' experiences.

DOMAINS OF EXPERIENCE

The coach considers six domains of a manager's experience as they have evolved over time (see Figure 12). The first three – role, skills and organisational context – provide the tangible business-relevant perspective.

The remaining three aspects are concerned with more personal elements of experience: personal circumstances, relationships and physical health. In practice these personal aspects are not explored in isolation, but are placed in the context of the career journey. In the assessing stage the coach makes a judgement about the degree to which some or all of these areas should be explored. Within each of these domains the coach shifts focus in relation to time, and also between high-level descriptions, and more detailed

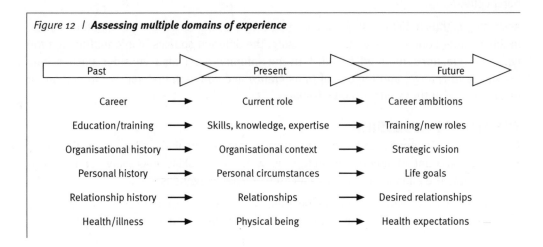

Figure 12 | *Assessing multiple domains of experience*

Past	Present	Future
Career	Current role	Career ambitions
Education/training	Skills, knowledge, expertise	Training/new roles
Organisational history	Organisational context	Strategic vision
Personal history	Personal circumstances	Life goals
Relationship history	Relationships	Desired relationships
Health/illness	Physical being	Health expectations

descriptions of events. It is the movement back and forth between different levels of description that enables the coach to categorise matters according to the ACE FIRST framework, and to understand its relevance to organisational goals.

SOURCES OF INFORMATION

The primary source of information for assessing comes from the coach's conversations with the manager. As I note below, both the content of conversations and the process of interaction that leads to certain disclosures or defences are aspects to which the coach pays attention and which can provide the essential basis for constructing a story of the manager's capacity to change. However, first I consider three other potential sources of information available to the coach:

- information from the sponsor
- feedback from colleagues
- information from psychometric questionnaires.

Information from the sponsor

Unless the manager is self-referred, a sponsor usually provides the initial information about the need for coaching. The sponsor is typically either the manager's boss, a human resource manager or a manager responsible for organising a programme of coaching for several managers. This initial information is vital because it provides an organisational perspective on the need for coaching. Without this information the coach must rely on the manager to describe the organisational priorities in which the coaching is being conducted. Unfortunately, managers undergoing coaching are not always well informed by others about how they are perceived to be performing, or the specific ways in which their contribution is expected to add value to the business. Sometimes this lack of feedback occurs because the sponsor is reluctant to confront an issue with the manager, but it is just as likely to be because the sponsor has not taken time to construct a clear purpose in his or her own mind for coaching. In these circumstances the assessing stage begins with 'coaching' the sponsor to be as clear as possible about the goals of coaching from his or her perspective.

When questioning the sponsor, in addition to understanding the broader context of the manager's role, the coach seeks to elicit a precise description of what the manager will be doing differently if the coaching is successful:

- What makes you think that coaching may be useful for this manager?
- What is the manager's role, and what are the key challenges of the role?
- How does the manager's role link with the wider goals of the department or organisation?
- In what ways is the manager performing well in the role?
- In what ways is the manager performing less well in the role?
- What is the most impressive or pleasantly surprising thing you have seen or heard from or about the manager recently?

- How will we know if the coaching has been successful? What specifically would you see the manager doing as a consequence of coaching?
- How do you wish to be kept informed about the manager's progress in coaching?

The discussion with the sponsor may also include consideration of whether other sources of information should be included as part of the coaching process – in particular the use of colleague feedback or the use of psychometric questionnaires.

Feedback from colleagues

The use of 360-degree feedback questionnaires, or interviews with colleagues (senior, peers, juniors and external contacts) either face-to-face or over the telephone, provides observer perceptions of a manager's performance and impact on others. In 360-degree feedback, perceptions of performance are rated against a set of behavioural competencies. In the case of colleague interviews, the coach asks questions that are similar to those posed to the sponsor, with the aim of identifying perceived strengths and weaknesses, and including detailed behavioural descriptions of what successful change would look like.

Feedback of this kind can be useful for encapsulating developmental challenges. But there are a number of reasons why such feedback must be used with caution.

First, if introduced too early into the coaching process, negative colleague feedback can undermine the creation of a positive learning space. The coach is perceived as the bringer of bad tidings, someone allied with a critical faction within the organisation, and so can evoke defensiveness from the manager.

Second, the quality of the feedback depends on the willingness of colleagues to be open in their provision of feedback. Colleagues, particularly junior staff, will be cautious about giving honest feedback if they believe the manager will guess its source and will harbour subsequent resentment towards them.

Third, in the case of 360-degree feedback the behavioural competencies rated within a questionnaire may not accurately reflect the critical aspects of leadership performance within the manager's role.

Overall, feedback from colleagues can add a useful dimension to the collection of information, but it must be viewed in the context of other information – in particular the coach's own direct experience of the manager.

Psychometric questionnaires

The underlying premise in psychometric questionnaires is that mental capacities and processes, personality and a range of behavioural styles can be distinguished and categorised. Such categorising provides a basis for measuring the traits of an individual, and for predicting how he or she is likely to perform in particular contexts. Intelligence and aptitude tests measure specific reasoning abilities and are often used to support assessment and selection in organisations. In coaching, psychometrics are used to indicate preferred styles in such areas as communication, decision-making, teamworking, emotional intelligence, interpersonal needs and relationship management. Understanding the implications of these preferences for a manager's work styles and relationships is a useful source of information for the coach. However, as I shall discuss in the next chapter, personality types and other psychometric results can seem to provide a fixed and deterministic picture of an individual, and so may seem to sanction existing behaviour rather than promote change. As to the use of 360-degree feedback, the coach has to decide if and when to introduce the results of psychometric questionnaires, taking account of the need to reinforce a person's capacity to change, as well as to acknowledge the limitations defined by his or her personality.

QUESTIONING

Effective questioning guides the process of reflection and discovery, steering the conversation, and giving shape and focus to new avenues of exploration. Further, questioning demonstrates the coach's interest and curiosity. The coach uses questioning to shift focus across a number of domains in order to build up a picture of the challenges and development opportunities available.

There are four groups of questions that the coach uses during assessing in order to guide the shifting focus of attention. These are:

- intention questions
- 'unpacking' questions
- possibility questions
- story questions.

Intention questions

Intention questions are designed to identify goals and outcomes. Intention questions elicit information at many levels, ranging from the furthest-reaching aspirations managers have for their lives, down to the specific details of what a manager will aim to do differently the very next day. The movement back and forth between high-level goals and specific measurable outcomes ensures that the purpose of a wide-ranging discussion is persistently connected with its relevance to improved business performance. These questions enable the coach to shape the manager's intentions, as described in Chapter 2.

Examples of high-level intention questions include:

- What do you want to achieve in your life?
- What is your personal vision or dream?
- What do you want to achieve in your work or organisation?
- What is the vision for the organisation?
- How does the vision for the organisation fit with your personal journey?
- Imagining that it is ten years hence and you are looking back on your achievements, what do you want to be able to see?

Questions that bring intentions to a more immediate level include:

- What achievable goals do you have for coaching?
- How will these goals connect with your broader vision for yourself and for the organisation?
- How will we know if coaching is successful?
- When the coaching is finished, what will be happening differently?
- What is the first sign that you will be able to notice that coaching has been helpful?

'Unpacking' questions

Unpacking questions provide detail and clarification. They are designed to take a broad statement and to 'unpack' the ACE FIRST constituents that are implicitly part of the statement. These questions are phrased to create the sense that any element is a changeable aspect of experience rather than an unchanging facet of personality.

Below are examples of questions associated with each element of the ACE FIRST model:

- What behaviours/thoughts/feelings have you found yourself using in relation to this situation? (questions about actions, cognitions and emotions)
- Where do you focus your attention in this kind of situation? (focus of attention)
- What do you expect to achieve by adopting this behaviour/way of thinking/feeling? (intentions)
- What is the consequence of adopting this behaviour/way of thinking/feeling? (results)
- What are the contexts in which you adopt this behaviour/way of thinking/feeling? (system)
- What physical experiences or tensions in your body do you associate with this circumstance? (tension)
- In what ways have these ways of being been learned through experience? (questions about the impact of history)

CASE STUDY

Gordon

Intention questions had identified that one of the development goals for Gordon was to improve his capacity to influence others in meetings. The following piece of dialogue from the assessing stage illustrates the use of intention and unpacking questions.

Coach: You have said that you want to be more effective in meetings. What would be the first thing that I would see happening if you were being more effective? [clarifying the intention]

CASE STUDY continued

Gordon:	Well, in meetings I find that I don't make the right kind of impact. To make a greater impact I need to say more. I know that – and yet when it comes to a meeting I don't seem to be able to do it.
C:	Can you illustrate what you mean with an example? When did that happen recently to you? [moving from a high-level story to a detailed description]
G:	Mmm . . . Let's think. I suppose it occurred only yesterday when I attended a project meeting. There were a number of important points that I wanted to raise about our development strategy, but they somehow got lost. The discussion got going and quite quickly there was tension between two of the people, who are at loggerheads about how to resolve an issue. I suppose this issue derailed the meeting, and the chairperson was not strong enough to get it back on track. As a senior manager in that group I should have done something constructive to address the situation.
C:	So this is as much about handling tension in meetings as it is about getting your contribution heard. Is that right? [clarifying the intention or desired outcome]
G:	A lot of our meetings become heated and it does make it hard to have constructive conversations. This has happened when I chair meetings as well.
C:	OK, so tell me what thoughts and feelings are evoked for you in this kind of situation? [probing to understand the manager's focus of attention within the ACE FIRST pattern]
G:	I don't know. I just think about the different points of view that are being expressed and try to decide the best way forward. Sometimes I make some notes, or look through some of the relevant papers that I have brought to the meeting.
C	*remains silent* [allowing the ACE FIRST pattern to be further unpacked]
G:	And yet I also think I should be doing something about this, taking a lead and finding a way of calming things down. It's just so difficult to do that in the heat of the moment. Afterwards I think about things that I might have said to help the discussion to be more constructive – but by then it is too late.
C:	Does this kind of meeting situation encourage particular feelings for you? [probing for emotions]
G:	Oh, I hate it. I feel frozen – I just don't want to be there.
C:	What do you think your reaction to this situation says about you? [exploring for self-awareness about the impact of emotions]
G:	I suppose I am not very good at handling confrontation. I always feel as if the whole thing is going to go totally out of control. And yet my boss believes that one of the roles of our department is to take a balanced view between the competing lobbies within the organisation and to broker constructive agreements.
C:	So, is this one of the ways in which your boss expects you to show greater influence? [probing to clarify the system in which the ACE FIRST pattern occurs and the organisational need already expressed by the boss]
G:	Yes, there is a great need in our business, particularly following the merger, to

manage new developments in a way that is logical and sensible, so that our strategy is not driven by one faction crushing another.

Using intention questions identified that managing interpersonal tension was a particular challenge for Gordon. Unpacking questions indicated that he became anxious in difficult meetings, but felt he should be able to handle these situations more constructively.

Possibility questions

Whereas managers may describe their experiences in terms of problems, possibility questions are specifically intended to shift focus to the ways in which managers are already successful. Possibility questions elicit information about effective ACE FIRST patterns, since assessing existing effectiveness indicates the inner resources that managers have for achieving their goals.

Examples of possibility questions include:

- What are the biggest successes in your career/life?
- When are you most effective at achieving specific goals?
- When did you approach this situation differently and get a different result?
- What behaviours/thoughts/feelings did you have when you achieved a more successful result?
- In what situations have you more easily achieved your intentions?
- How do you feel in your body when you achieve your intentions?

Gordon, *continued*

Coach: You have described how you tend to withdraw in meetings when tensions are running high, and that although you feel you should be taking control of the situation, a fear of confrontation looms up in front of you and stops you from taking action. Can you think of situations of confrontation in your life where this does not occur – where, despite a fear, you have managed to take control of the situation?

Gordon: Well, what springs to mind are arguments between the kids. When they clash I usually handle the situation very rationally. In fact, I have managed to do that with my team members as well. Where I find it most difficult is with managers from other departments.

C: So, in many situations you are really quite good at managing tensions. If you think back, how well did you do this when you first managed a team?

G: Oh, I hated conflict then as well, and probably didn't cope very well. But gradually,

CASE STUDY continued

through experience, I have learned that if you understand enough about what is behind people's opposition, then you can begin to see how to find a solution.

Using possibility questions Gordon identified a prior occasion where he had managed to overcome the fear of confrontation. Unpacking questions applied to this experience were then used to understand the effective ACE FIRST pattern, and to explore how to apply this effective pattern to other meeting situations.

Story questions

In shifting focus to the past the coach invites managers to tell a story, drawing out key events in their lives or careers. In approaching history, coaches identify themes that help to make sense of the managers' developmental challenges. One way into their personal stories is to ask them to draw a lifeline, so that the ups and downs of life over time are plotted on a graph. Another method is to ask managers to draw a relationship tree, showing their key relationships. In both cases these are tools to encourage managers to tell a story about their experiences, and to begin to see patterns and links.

Useful questions for eliciting a manager's story include:

- I would now like to understand something of your history, both personally and in your career. As you talk about these, I am interested in those experiences or relationships that have been most formative for you. Where would you like to start?

- Tell me about your early life. How many children were there in your family? Where were you in the birth order?

- How would you describe your relationship with your mother/father/siblings?

- In what ways have those relationships/experiences influenced your outlook on life?

- Looking back over your life, what are the achievements of which you are most proud?

- What are the experiences that you found most challenging?

As managers tell a story about their lives and careers, the coach uses unpacking questions to gain more detail about a particular experience, or possibility questions to reinforce abilities that have proved most useful. As the story evolves, the coach looks for links between the past, present and future, and starts to build a story about the manager's journey and development challenges.

CASE STUDY

Gordon, *continued*

In response to a broad open question about his early experiences, Gordon described his background as a happy one. He was the eldest of two brothers, brought up in a middle-class family. His father was a manager within a local firm and his mother looked after Gordon and his brother. He described his mother as caring, and his father as a role model of integrity. In the context of Gordon's desire to be more assertive in meetings when tensions were running high, I wanted to unpack his experience of these relationships, particularly that with his father.

Coach: Can you tell me more about how you experienced your relationship with your father?

Gordon: Sure – what do you want to know? I suppose my mother was more involved with us on a day-to-day basis, but he was a very reassuring influence. He was an organised person who had a clear sense of how things should be done. Not that he told us what to do, but I did not want to make a fuss.

C: What do you mean by that?

G: Well, he always seemed so dignified that we didn't want to cause trouble or upset him. Don't get me wrong – I am not saying that we couldn't play around and be boisterous like any kids, but he did like us to be reasonable.

C: What would not being reasonable mean?

G: He didn't like it if we argued or had fights – but then again, what parent does?

C: So what would happen if you did argue or fight?

G: *(thinks for a while)* Well, he wouldn't get angry. It was more that he seemed hurt by the fact that we were not being dignified.

C: How did he give you that sense of him being hurt?

G: I don't know, really. I suppose he just looked sort of disappointed. You know – his mouth would turn down and he would take a deep breath. And sometimes he would just walk away.

C: I wonder what feelings were evoked in you when you saw this response?

G: I didn't like it . . . I felt as if I had let him down, as if I was being petty and childish. I suppose he was quite disapproving, even if silently so.

C: What thoughts do you imagine were going through your mind when he behaved like that?

G: Well, partly I felt responsible because I was the eldest and my parents did expect me to set an example. My brother was only a couple of years younger, but he did seem to get away with things more. I suppose I thought I should be a prefect at home as well as at school.

C: What would that mean doing?

G: That would mean me telling my brother to calm down and to be careful. It would mean stopping him from messing about or always wanting to romp and fight. He was a bit of a rebel. He got into trouble quite a lot at school.

C: And what about the rebel in you?

G: No, I wasn't a rebel.

The dialogue illustrates how I sought to explore a specific aspect of Gordon's history, because it seemed to be providing a clue to his fear of confrontation in meetings. This case study is taken up again in the next chapter as part of the task of story-making.

ASSESSING UNCONSCIOUS FACTORS

Thus far I have described the aims of assessing, the domains of experience about which we are seeking to gain information, the sources of that information, and the main types of questions we can ask to elicit that information. So long as the manager is open and collaborative, this process can proceed easily. However, in reality a manager's attitude to change is more complex because, as we have explored in earlier chapters, unconscious factors can create a resistance to change.

To work with unconscious factors the coach needs to have a method for gaining access to unconscious material. First and foremost this means that the coach must be vigilant to the nuances and details of interpersonal experience, looking for indicative signs of how managers relate, but of which they are unaware.

For example, the coach may experience a manager as flooding the session with detail, making it impossible to identify key patterns, or preventing the coach from having space to comment. Or the coach may experience the manager as being persistently flippant, defusing every serious point with a joke. Or the coach may notice that the manager is constantly blaming others or the organisation for problems. Or the coach may notice how the manager sits rigidly still, tense and constrained. These and other behaviours may indicate the use of unconscious defences, and the coach has then to consider what unconscious agenda may be driving this defensive behaviour.

The examination of the manager's ACE FIRST patterns encourages such vigilance, because it suggests that all behaviour, including defensive behaviour, is part of a learned pattern that will have conscious and unconscious aspects. The challenge for the coach is to interpret these patterns. Within leadership coaching there are two linked areas of focus for developing an understanding of unconscious issues: the transference and the countertransference.

TRANSFERENCE

Transference has already been examined as one of the core aspects of psychoanalytic theory – the concept that past experiences are unconsciously triggered and re-enacted in the present (see Chapter 3). At this stage I want to explore a particular kind of transference – namely, the here-and-now transference that occurs directly in relation to the coach.

The idea here is that managers cannot help but deal with their relationship with the coach in the same way that they deal with other relationships and circumstances in their lives.

Thus the unconscious issues that underpin their leadership behaviours will also impinge on their interactions with a coach. For example, managers who refuse to engage with the emotional concerns of staff due to a denial of their own emotional issues are likely to expect a coach to move practically from one issue to another without dwelling on what feelings these issues evoke. The coach's experience may be one of being railroaded along. Managers transfer their behaviour from their working environment to the coaching environment. Furthermore, the coach may realise that the pressure to be practical is part of a pattern of being and relating that stems from a complexity of interactions, initially with parents in childhood, and reinforced or modified by a multiplicity of subsequent interactions.

In talking about the transference, then, we may describe managers as *transferring* certain past experiences into their leadership roles, and into their relationships with their coaches. Such formulations are not intended to reduce behaviour to a mechanical account of action and reaction. Rather, they are intended to distil out the subtle ways in which personality and environment (and particularly early environment) combine to shape behaviour, and to exemplify how managers unconsciously transfer these complex patterns of being and relating into the coaching setting.

To understand the transference the coach can (privately) consider three questions:

- What is the behaviour that I can see and hear that suggests the operation of unconscious defences, and in particular, transference?

- What is the transference story? What aspect of the manager is being projected onto me? What do I represent in the manager's past?

- What are the implications of this story in terms of the manager's unconscious agenda?

The here-and-now transference can take numerous forms, and it may involve considerable conscious work on the part of the coach to understand it – a successful manager's defences are usually highly effective. Table 11 illustrates three possible transference stories based on the attachment patterns and leadership styles described in Chapter 3. During the assessing stage the transference is examined in order to make sense of the unconscious agenda, and any interpretation remains, at least initially, unspoken. The construction is used to inform the coach's story-making (Stage 3 in the coaching process) about the manager's capacity for change. The coach decides if and when to interpret the unconscious agenda as part of a decision about what is necessary to enable useful change. Interpretations based on the transference are often useful for reframing (Stage 5 in the coaching process), even though the coach never refers directly to the unconscious agenda.

COUNTERTRANSFERENCE

The concept of countertransference – as an unconscious communication from the manager to the coach – was introduced in Chapter 3. This phenomenon is of particular relevance within the assessing stage of coaching, since it provides the coach with

Table 11 | Leadership styles and possible transference

Leadership style	Observation	Transference story	Unspoken interpretation
Authentic	Manager is self-disclosing and open to feedback.	Coach is a collaborative and discerning friend.	Manager is likely to work productively. Unconscious causes little obstacle.
Defiant	Manager is guarded, or critical.	Coach is either a critical parent, or if reversed, a disappointing child.	Feelings of vulnerability and neediness may underlie unconscious resistance.
Compliant	Manager is friendly and keen to please, or overly formal and transactional.	Coach is an unreliable parent, potentially conspiratorial and/or distant.	Feelings of frustration and fear of spontaneity may underlie resistance.

invaluable information about possible areas of unconscious resistance. However, this concept perhaps more than any other from the world of psychotherapy can seem alien and even mystical to the world of business. How is it, the pragmatist will say, that one person's unconscious can communicate with another person's unconscious? The answer lies in the nuances of behaviour, movements, mannerisms, facial expressions, the tone of voice, the use of words and the many other subtleties of interaction that are unconsciously expressed by one person and unconsciously perceived by another.[1] Drawing on our evolutionary heritage, we can sense much more about other people than our conscious minds are able to process.

In leadership coaching we can come to know something about a manager's unconscious experience by attending to the feelings and reactions that arise within ourselves, but that nevertheless seem relevant to the manager.

Countertransference as intrusion

However, working with the countertransference is not easy. Coaches may not be able to distinguish between feelings that derive from a manager's unconscious and those that derive from their own unconscious. Managers may trigger unresolved issues and concerns in the coach that intrude on the coach's capacity to work effectively with the manager. This can occur because the coach's unconscious contains personal conflictual issues that he or she would rather not face or take responsibility for. In attributing his or her own conflictual feelings to the manager, a coach may unconsciously use the countertransference as a means of projecting personal emotional blind spots onto the manager. In such cases we can think of countertransference as an intrusion into the work of coaching.

For example, a coach may have learned to cope with feelings of self-doubt by suppressing them and presenting a façade of confident professionalism. However, when working with a confident manager the coach's suppressed self-doubt may be felt more acutely. In order to maintain a sense of control the coach may unconsciously seek to undermine the confidence of the manager, such that the coach retains a sense of being the expert. In this sense the coach's countertransference, which remains unconscious, is an intrusion that undermines the work of coaching.

Countertransference as indicator

On the other hand, if coaches, drawing on self-awareness and reflection, can distinguish their own unconscious issues from those of managers, then the countertransference can be an indicator of unconscious issues in managers that would otherwise remain inaccessible.

For example, a manager may deny feelings of self-doubt about leadership competence by presenting a façade of confidence. In coaching, the manager may unconsciously project this self-doubt onto the coach, and at the same time make undermining comments to the coach. The net effect is that the coach experiences feelings of self-doubt that have their root in the manager's self-doubt. In this case the experience of self-doubt is an example of countertransference as indicator. The importance of this experience is that if the coach can become aware of it, and subject it to inner scrutiny, it is a valuable source of information about the manager's unconscious feelings.

The reality of working with the countertransference

The idea that the coach's countertransference is never an intrusion is in fact unrealistic. In my experience, I, and those I have supervised, are continually tripping over our tendencies to react, to project, or to defend, based on our own unconscious issues. Whether we respond with impatience, competitiveness, formality, seductiveness or caution, these and many other reactions can derive from our own unconscious patterns of relating. Although a coach's self-awareness and experience can do much to pre-empt such reactions, it is often those unconscious reactions that we do not recognise until afterwards that are most telling. By reflecting about the meaning of reactions that have already played out, coaches can come to understand the complexity of the unconscious agenda.

In practice such unconscious reactions are usually not wholly countertransference as intrusion nor wholly countertransference as indicator, but a combination of the two. It is in recognising the intrusion of their own unconscious reactions, and then looking for possible unconscious triggers in the behaviour of the manager, that coaches can convert the intrusive countertransference into an indicator.

> **CASE STUDY**
>
> **Working with the countertransference**
>
> A coach had developed a trusting and productive relationship with a manager, who had explored the development of his assertiveness in relation to members of the board. Towards the end of the coaching assignment they began to review the degree to which the manager's behaviour had changed. On hearing the coach's account of this review, two things struck me. First, although the manager had gained important insights about himself, he was not translating these insights into practical change. Second, the coach was not tackling this shortfall in practical change, and focused more on celebrating the personal insights that the manager had gained. It seemed to me that the coach was unconsciously colluding with the manager to avoid the discomfort of confrontation.
>
> In discussion it became apparent that the coach himself had a tendency to accommodate, and to this extent his avoidance of the shortfalls in the manager's realisation of change represented countertransference as intrusion. The coach's own unconscious defence against expressing frustration and self-assertion were intruding in the work. However, the coach's unconscious reaction was not solely his own. It was fuelled by the manager's unconscious fear of confrontation, as evidenced by the many ways in which he complied with others in order to maintain harmony. Thus the manager was creating an unconscious pressure on the coach to turn a blind eye to the core development issue, and this aspect represented countertransference as indicator.
>
> Distinguishing the countertransference reactions, the intrusion and the indicator, the coach realised that he was being unduly cautious. He had to show the manager that they could have a frank discussion about the outstanding need for change, and that such a discussion did not have to become aggressive or traumatising. By being conscious of the countertransference he could notice the unconscious pull to repeating, within the coaching relationship, a collusive compliance.
>
> Sorting out the 'intrusive' and 'indicating' aspects of the countertransference enabled the coach to make interventions that evoked the manager's capacity for interpersonal resilience, and so move towards his career goals with greater awareness and authenticity.

The assessment of the countertransference, and the degree to which it is an intrusion or indicator, is one of the crucial areas for consideration in supervision (Chapter 9). The main safeguard against an abuse of the countertransference is the capacity for coaches to reflect on their reactions and to become more conscious. I have found it useful to guide this process of reflection by considering the following questions:

- What is the countertransference experience? What do I feel/think/do that is distinctive and specifically linked to being with this manager? (To what extent is this experience more about me than it is about the manager?)

Table 12 | Leadership styles and possible countertransference

Leadership style	Countertransference experience	Coach's unconscious reaction	Unspoken interpretation
Authentic	Sense of competence and productivity	Confident, attuned, sustaining the learning space	Unconscious issues are not prevalent or disruptive
Defiant	Feeling rejected, useless, or unprofessional.	Trying to prove oneself or defensively competing with the manager	Coach is experiencing manager's unconscious fear of rejection
Compliant	Enjoying the intimacy but frustrated by transactional detail	Conspiratorial attitude switching to guilty action planning	Coach is experiencing manager's denial of frustration mixed with a desire to be good

- How do I find myself reacting in a way that is distinctive and specific to this manager, and that is not a result of my own unconscious issues?
- What are the implications of this countertransference experience and my unconscious reaction for understanding the manager's unconscious experience?

Table 12 illustrates three countertransference (as indicator) stories based on the attachment patterns and leadership styles discussed in Chapter 3. Comparing Tables 11 and 12, we can see that the transference and the countertransference are usually linked, because it is a manager's transference to the coach that evokes the coach's countertransference. So, for example, a rejected manager transfers this experience onto the coach by being subtly rejecting, and then the coach may feel rejected and worthless as a reaction to the manager's unconscious experience. Able to think about these feelings, the coach gains experiential insight into feelings that are unconscious for the manager.

Summary

In the assessing stage the coach gathers information about the manager's career and life journey, sometimes drawing on several sources of information, including feedback from the sponsor, from colleagues and from psychometric questionnaires.

In coaching conversations, questioning is the essential tool for guiding the process of reflection and discovery, and questions are used to shift focus across different domains of the manager's experience, across time from present to future to past, and between high-level and more detailed descriptions of experience and aspirations. Questions used in the assessing stage fall into four primary groups – intention, unpacking, possibility and story questions – and these are combined to construct a story of the manager's development challenges.

The coach also has to assess attitudes to change, in particular identifying defensiveness and unconscious resistance to change. An understanding of the manager's unconscious agenda can be developed through working with the processes of transference and countertransference.

ENDNOTE

1 The psychoanalyst Wilfred Bion (1961, 1962) powerfully illustrates the roots of the countertransference experience. He notes that when a baby cries, a mother can actually feel the baby's distress. The cry evokes distress in the mother, which motivates her to think about what is causing the baby's distress, and then to take action to relieve it. The mother's experience of distress is an example of countertransference. However, making sense of this experience is not simple. In the case of the baby's distress, the mother's feelings and reactions will be influenced by (his or) her own capacity to deal with anxiety. An anxious mother may attribute a degree of distress to the baby that is much greater than what the baby is actually experiencing, and so the mother may be intrusively attentive to the baby. On the other hand the mother may cope with the baby's real distress by denying her own anxiety, as well as the baby's, and so may respond in a brusque and unsympathetic way. The capacity of a mother to be open to the baby's real distress and to know it for what it is, requires that she has a degree of self-awareness about her own typical levels of anxiety. The act of thinking about feelings and distinguishing what belongs to the baby and what belongs to the mother is the same process as that required for making sense of the countertransference

6

Story-making

The universe is made of stories, not of atoms.

Muriel Rukeyser (1913–1980)

The third and central stage within the LASER coaching process is *story-making*. Following the establishment of *the learning space*, and the collection of information during the *assessing* stage, the coach seeks to construct a meaningful story to make sense of the developmental challenges facing managers. Stories serve as provisional hypotheses about why people behave as they do – what motivates them, what trips them up, what choices they are likely to make, what blind spots they have. Working to construct coherent stories, coaches are forced to be conscious about their approach, and to test their hypotheses systematically. Further, a story enables coaches to predict how managers will learn, and to align their interventions with these hypotheses.

Underpinning the concept of story-making[1] is an emphasis on two areas:

- the need for the coach to consider multiple perspectives
- the need to view story-making as arising out of the conversation between coach and manager.

MULTIPLE PERSPECTIVES

The hypotheses that coaches formulate are implicitly influenced by established mindsets. Often this means viewing coaching from a single perspective. A coach who usually thinks in terms of developing effective behaviours will thus tend to construct the coaching challenge in terms of the need to clarify goals and required behaviours. A coach trained in cognitive techniques will construct the coaching challenge in terms of beliefs. A coach trained in psychodynamics will construct the coaching challenge in terms of unconscious issues and the need to surface unconscious blocks. A coach trained in systemic thinking will construct the coaching challenge in terms of the social and cultural factors that are shaping the manager's capacity to change.

The ACE FIRST model of change explicitly seeks to encourage coaches to construct stories from multiple perspectives – to see the similarities and inconsistencies between different viewpoints, and to reflect on the implications of these different patterns of meaning for facilitating change. However, as I have highlighted already in Chapter 2, the ACE FIRST model itself could be viewed as just one particular perspective. As such it must also be used consciously, with an eye to how it can hinder as much as help the coaching process. In story-making the aim is to invite a willingness to pull the rug away from our own perceptions, to notice the biases, limitations and possibilities in one way of seeing compared to another.

STORY-MAKING THROUGH CONVERSATION

The realities that managers take for granted are the realities that they have been surrounded by since birth, in their family, in their culture, in their multiple roles, in their careers. These realities provide the beliefs, practices, words and experiences from which people author their lives. Coaching is an invitation to managers to 're-story' their realities, to use conversation and collaboration to reframe their self-narratives and the possibilities they can realise.

Although certain aspects of story-making are an unspoken construction held in the mind of the coach, its creation and ongoing re-authoring is the product of conversations between the coach and the manager. The kinds of questions that the coach asks affects the response, and the response affects further questions. It is within the interplay of dialogue, and out of the tension of silences, that new plots and characters can emerge. Such a view challenges the idea that the coach holds the answers and simply decides when and how to dispense them. Rather, it encourages the coach to view the story as jointly authored through the unravelling interchange of conversation.

An ACE FIRST pattern describes a particular way of being. A story, then, is an ACE FIRST pattern that extends through time. Through the process of habit and unconscious repetition the ACE FIRST story may come to represent certain self-narratives, some useful and some limiting. In working with an ACE FIRST story, the coach and manager seek to understand how specific elements of experience have contributed to these narratives, and so understand how the ACE FIRST story can be re-authored with new possibilities.

A story's usefulness

In that no story corresponds to the truth, the value of any particular story depends on its usefulness. Although a story is constructed within the relationship between coach and

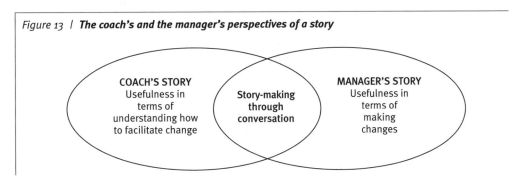

Figure 13 | *The coach's and the manager's perspectives of a story*

COACH'S STORY
Usefulness in terms of understanding how to facilitate change

Story-making through conversation

MANAGER'S STORY
Usefulness in terms of making changes

manager, the particular perspective that the coach and manager have of the story and of the way in which that perspective can be useful is not the same. The usefulness of the coach's perspective of the story is that it indicates what the coach might do to facilitate change. The usefulness of a manager's perspective is that it enables him or her to make changes (see Figure 13).

In story-making we are concerned with the coach's perspective, since it is at this stage that the coach is constructing a basis for making choices about useful interventions. In the reframing stage we are more concerned with the manager's perspective, since it is at that stage that the responsibility for embracing change is passed to the manager.

Although there are many ways of constructing stories that are useful to the coach, in this chapter I consider five approaches that emphasise different elements of the ACE FIRST model of change. These are:

- the systemic story
- the cognitive story
- the history story
- the personality story
- the relationship story.

THE SYSTEMIC STORY

The systemic story is concerned with the way in which the organisational context, and specific relationships within that context, is influencing the capacity of managers to achieve their goals. This story is based primarily on three elements of the ACE FIRST framework – the *system*, *intentions* and *results*. Focusing on these three elements invites the coach to consider how the pressures and organisational demands of a manager's role (system) structure the setting and measurement of goals (intentions and results).

For example, if there is an organisational need for high-quality project management, an individual manager is more likely to be assigned objectives associated with project management, and coaching has to take account of this organisational need. Furthermore, the training of project managers, the experience of bosses in relation to project management, and the degree of realism in evaluating the performance of project managers, will all play their part in making sense of the systemic story. Questioning to build the systemic story involves understanding how the coach's work objectives have been framed, and how multiple agendas within the organisation contribute to this framing.

We can think of the systemic story as containing two aspects – a conscious agenda and an unconscious agenda. The conscious agenda of the systemic story is in many ways similar to a performance appraisal. In performance appraisal a boss assesses a person's performance in terms of his or her achievement of specific goals, and these goals are consciously linked to the organisational purpose. However, the degree to which these goals are achieved, and the way in which their achievement is evaluated, is influenced as much by unconscious factors as conscious ones. A boss's strengths and weaknesses as a manager, and as a developer of others, can have a significant impact on a person's performance, as can a boss's handling of pressures from his or her own boss. Probing to understand these underlying issues and contexts enables the coach to construct a systemic story, and so to consider interventions that address a manager's context as much as the personal dimensions of change.

CASE STUDY

Nick

Nick received coaching as part of a senior manager development initiative. When he started coaching he had been an area manager for nine months, reporting in to his regional manager, and his promising performance led him to be nominated for the coaching programme. However, in looking at his *intentions*, *results* and the *system*, Nick's coach constructed a story that highlighted a crucial challenge for Nick's further development.

Nick was ambitious and his personal goal was to excel in his new role, to receive the highest grading in his performance review, and so to be considered for promotion in the next round of career reviews. Yet in due course his performance review, although very positive, marked him down on his handling of difficult members of staff because he had struggled to work effectively with his deputy. The coach had explored Nick's managerial style and it did seem that he could be brusque with those who were not self-motivated. But the difficulty with the deputy owed as much to the complexity of the system as it did to Nick's management style.

It transpired that the deputy – a man 10 years older than Nick – had been demoted from the area manager role following a disappointing performance. He had been offered a deputy role in another office, but he had chosen to stay in the same office that he had formerly managed because it was close to where he and his family lived. Furthermore, the regional manager and the deputy had known each other a long time, had been through many organisational changes together, and wanted to remain on good terms despite the problems of performance that had arisen.

The coach's story of this situation combined an understanding of Nick's intentions, the evaluation of his results, and the systemic factors in which he was operating (see Figure 14). From the outset Nick had been placed in a highly problematic role in relation to his deputy, whom he had replaced. The coach hypothesised that the regional manager had himself been pushed, by his own boss, into demoting the former area manager, and that the regional manager was reluctant to be tough with the deputy. He was therefore passing the buck to Nick. In that the deputy had been specifically allowed to remain within the same area, Nick had been set up to fail by his boss, however unconsciously.

Nick's performance goal was to elicit high-quality productivity from the deputy – something that the regional manager himself had failed to do. Nick, in buying in to this goal, had taken on an unrealistic expectation.

Figure 14 | **The systemic story for Nick**

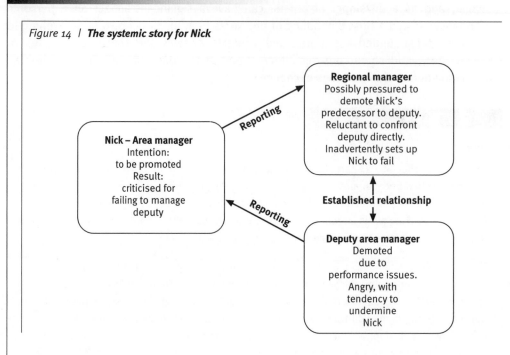

This construction provided the coach with a basis for considering a number of interventions. For example, the coach considered how Nick could negotiate with his boss about his performance, reassessing the achievability of intentions and results in a way that took account of the intrinsically problematic management challenge. The coach also considered how getting Nick to deepen his understanding of the relationship between the deputy and the regional manager could enable him to understand the political context in which he was being judged.

THE COGNITIVE STORY

In developing the cognitive story the coach seeks to identify characteristic patterns of thinking and to understand how these impact on a manager's performance. The way in which managers think about themselves or others begins to be revealed as soon as they start to talk. Their use of language, their styles of expression, and their statements about future possibilities indicate how they make sense of experiences. Implicit within their language are the cognitive rules, attitudes and beliefs that govern their self-narratives. These rules can be enabling or limiting, and understanding when and how they are applied constitutes the cognitive story.

Enabling and limiting cognitions

Some of the common enabling and limiting cognitions revealed through the manager's language are shown in Table 13.

Table 13 | *Enabling and limiting cognitions*

Enabling	Limiting
BALANCED THINKING: 'My occasional mistakes show me how to improve.'	ALL-OR-NOTHING THINKING: 'A mistake shows I'm a failure.'
POSITIVE PROPHECY: 'I believe they will like it/it will go well.'	NEGATIVE PROPHECY: 'I am bound to get it wrong.'
PRECISION THINKING: 'There are two issues we need to address.'	OVER-GENERALISATION/EXAGGERATION: 'Everything is going wrong today [based on one or two things going wrong].'
RATIONAL REASONING: 'My anxiety says more about me than it does about others.'	EMOTIONAL REASONING: 'I feel anxious, so they are bound to be critical.'
VALUING THE POSITIVE: 'That was a real achievement of which I am proud.'	DISCOUNTING THE POSITIVE: 'Anyone could have done what I did.'
CHECKING OUT: 'What did you like most/least about it?'	MIND READING: 'They thought I was terrible' [without checking it out with them].'

'Balanced thinking' occurs when someone makes a measured judgement about a situation. For example, thinking about a competitor a manager might say, 'Their success shows that we need to get better at canvassing wider opinion.' This way of thinking is enabling because it helps the manager to move forward in a constructive way. In contrast 'all-or-nothing thinking' is polarised, so the manager might say, 'Our loss of this contract shows we are useless.' All-or-nothing thinking is limiting in the sense that it leaves the manager with nowhere to go, and fragile in the face of anything that is not perfect.

A 'positive prophecy' refers to the belief that something in the future will go well, whereas a 'negative prophecy' assumes that something will not go well, and these expectations influence actions, emotions and ultimately the result.

'Precision thinking' is contrasted with 'over-generalisation' or 'exaggeration'. Like balanced thinking, precision thinking provides a basis for understanding what is working and what is not working, whereas generalisation and exaggeration create either vagueness or an attitude of absolutes that invites defeatism in the face of setbacks.

'Rational reasoning' is an aspect of self-awareness, where a person examines his or her feelings without assuming that these feelings are a guide to the external world. In 'emotional reasoning' personal feelings are assumed to be an indication of external reality – so, for example, anxiety before a presentation may be read as indicating a real threat from the audience, even though the audience is benign or possibly friendly.

'Valuing and discounting the positive', which are, respectively, the enabling and limiting facets of the same cognitive area, refers to people's attitude towards their achievements.

People who value and celebrate their positive achievements are more likely to build and sustain a healthy self-esteem. Conversely, people who dismiss their achievements, or focus on failures, are more likely to undermine their self-esteem. The coach can readily gauge the attitude of managers towards their own achievements by providing positive feedback and noting how they respond.

'Checking out' refers to a belief that we cannot know what others are thinking about us unless we ask them. The need to elicit and clarify feedback from others through active questioning is an essential basis for gaining an objective understanding of others' perceptions. 'Mind reading', in contrast, refers to the belief that we know what someone else is thinking. Whether we assume those thoughts are positive or negative, without checking out we are likely to have a limited understanding of others' perceptions.

Cognitive stories and leadership style

In practice, the language of managers reveals a mixture of attitudes and beliefs about themselves and others. Typically, there are many aspects of thinking that are enabling, as well as some that are more limiting. In building the cognitive story the coach seeks to identify patterns of thinking and to understand how these patterns are influencing behaviour.

I have distinguished three leadership styles – authentic, defiant and compliant leadership. In terms of the cognitive story, the manager who shows authentic leadership demonstrates a greater proportion of enabling cognitions, which are linked to positive actions and emotions. Evidence, for example, of balanced thinking, rational reasoning and a willingness to check out feedback thus suggests an enabling cognitive story, in which the manager has a fair degree of self-awareness, and potentially the capacity for authentic leadership. In contrast, a manager who shows a more defiant or compliant leadership style uses certain limiting cognitions, and these will be linked with problematic actions and emotions.

Core beliefs

In developing the cognitive story it is useful to differentiate cognitions according to the degree to which they are unconscious. Those that are most readily available to awareness are spontaneous thoughts – the verbal messages that flash through the mind. At a deeper level, but less available to awareness, are attitudes or long-held assumptions that are deeply ingrained. Furthest out of awareness are core beliefs – deeply embedded unconscious mindsets that influence a person's self-narratives and sense of identity. The cognitive story is obtained by the coach listening for the verbalisation of spontaneous thoughts, and treating them as clues to deeper attitudes and beliefs. By asking repetitively probing questions about what spontaneous thoughts mean for a manager, the coach can gradually bring to the surface deeper attitudes and core beliefs (Greenberger and Padesky, 1995).

THE HISTORY STORY

In constructing a story based on history the coach is looking for patterns that make sense of a person's present-day experiences. History provides the context and background for a personal story, indicating how managers achieve certain goals, but also how they are blocked from achieving other goals.

In the history story the coach maps ACE FIRST patterns through time, identifying how a range of experiences are being replayed, consciously or unconsciously, in the present.

Linking past and present

The construction of the content of the history story occurs in parallel with the questioning process within the assessing stage of coaching. It is through the coach's curiosity that the manager is guided to recall and put words to experiences. The coach invites the manager to provide a rich account of events and relationships that might not have been thought about for many years, if ever. The use of unpacking and story-making questions (see Chapter 5) brings the manager's memories to the surface, and the coach's hypotheses about what these memories indicate provides the basis for further questions from the coach.

For example, a manager describing her success as captain of a regional hockey team led her coach to hypothesise that she has a strong drive to succeed and to be in control. The coach then asked questions to understand more about why she chose hockey, how she became captain, what it feels like if she is not captain, what motivated her to go to regular hockey training. Each question sought to shed light on the burgeoning story, which is gradually built into a more coherent account of learning based on past experiences.

There are three aspects of the manager's personal descriptions that the coach uses to construct the content of the history story:

- past experiences
- learning from those experiences
- the result of that learning in the present.

In looking at past experiences, the coach considers both rewarding and difficult experiences. The unpacking of those experiences in terms of ACE FIRST patterns provides indications of conscious and unconscious learning. The result of those experiences in the present is constructed by looking for links between patterns of learning and their re-enactment in the present. In my experience it is surprising how often resonance between past and present experiences, which seem transparently obvious once identified, have not been seen before. The link has not been made because it is held unconsciously out of awareness.

This was certainly true in a brief piece of coaching with Charles.

CASE STUDY

Charles

This illustration is based not on a sustained piece of coaching, but on a couple of conversations with a manager during a two-day workshop. Within the workshop, participants were expected to make a presentation. Charles raised alarm at the idea of giving a presentation, something he avoided like the plague, and his colleagues on the workshop confirmed that this was Charles's Achilles heel.

I decided to take him aside for 20 minutes to see if I could uncover why a successful team leader had such problems with presentations. I asked him what happens in presentations. He said that in the middle of important presentations to senior managers he suddenly loses his way, digresses, becomes self-conscious, and ultimately fails to deliver a clear message. I asked him what triggered this behaviour (ie what was the context for this ineffective ACE pattern). He said he seemed to derail in his presentations when he perceived the audience as blank and disengaged, and felt they were thinking critically about him (possibly a limiting cognition of 'mind-reading').

Deciding to explore the history story, I asked him about his relationship with his parents, and probed to understand key aspects of his learning from these relationships. He recalled his father as encouraging him to take on challenges and helping him to believe in himself. These recollections helped to make sense of his confidence and his capacity to motivate members of his team. However, he described his mother as a more practical person who needed to be in control within the home, and who expected Charles to fit in a good deal. Charles would assert himself with his mother, fighting for the things he wanted to do, but would often be greeted with a powerful and disapproving silence. This silence would then be followed by expressions of disappointment and dismissive withdrawal.

I asked Charles how these episodes made him feel. He said he felt a mixture of anger, guilt and shame – angry for not being supported, and guilty and ashamed at not being an obedient son who followed his mother's wishes. His response to his mother's silent disapproval was to keep talking, both to fill the silence and to put off his mother's disappointment when she did finally comment.

It seemed to me that Charles's experience of his mother's silent disapproval provided a compelling history story for what was happening in important presentations.

Charles perceived blankness from his audience as disapproval, based on a projection of his experience of his mother's silent disapproval. His response to this projection was to speak too much in order to fill the silence. However, his self-consciousness meant that he would lose his way, he would start to digress, he would perceive his audience as becoming more frustrated or critical, and he would become self-critical. Consequently, his experience of himself derailing during a presentation seemed to be triggered by his unconscious projection of disapproval.

CASE STUDY continued

Despite having attended presentation skills workshops and personal development workshops Charles had never made this link. The unconscious feelings associated with this insight had held it out of awareness as a resistance to linking.

THE PERSONALITY STORY

There are a number of theories of personality that seek to make sense of the similarities and differences between people. These theories can be broadly differentiated in terms of the nature/nurture debate – the degree to which personality is viewed as either a product of natural disposition or a result of environmental experiences. Our view of this question is important because it influences our approach to coaching. If for example we believe we are dealing with a natural, relatively unchanging facet of personality, then coaching will focus on helping the manager to recognise and come to terms with this bias, and with understanding how to manage associated strengths and weaknesses. On the other hand, if we believe we are dealing with a learned aspect of behaviour, coaching will focus on challenging the usefulness of this learning and seek to enable more fundamental change.

Authenticity and personality

In developing authentic leadership it may be tempting to equate the idea of authenticity with that of personality. According to this view, authenticity would be the expression of individual personality, and the coach's role would be to identify and to encourage that personality to be freely expressed. However, in my view the concept of personality must be understood in a similar way to that of authentic leadership.

Just as authentic leadership is not exclusively concerned with individual expression, but with the tension between the individual and the organisation, so personality is always the result of the interaction between genes and the environment (Plomin, 1994; Loehlin, 1992; Eaves et al, 1989). Certain facets of personality, such as emotional stability (ie calmness v anxiousness) or social adaptability (ie extroversion v introversion), may thus be viewed as genetic predispositions, but these predispositions are powerfully shaped from birth onwards by social and cultural influences. A description of personality is always a story about how certain intrinsic biases and predispositions have interacted with extrinsic circumstances to create the uniqueness of self-identity. The authentic expression of personality is a creation, a story arising from the ongoing interaction of predisposition and experience.

Preference and psychological type

In developing the personality story a useful concept is that of psychological types, as introduced by Carl Jung (1971) – the idea that a person has particular preferences for the way he or she perceives and makes judgements about the world. Drawing on Jung's theory of type, psychometrics have been developed that describe personality as a profile of preferences on each of four dimensions: extroversion-introversion, practical-creative (sensing-intuition), thinking-feeling and structured-flexible (judging-perceiving).[2]

Such profiles can be very helpful in coaching because they provide a ready-made story of the likely qualities and characteristics of managers. Indeed, many managers are impressed by the descriptive clarity contained within their personality profile, and gain awareness about themselves and their differences from others. However, a profile may also be viewed as a limiting and deterministic label that encourages managers to reconcile themselves to defined ways of being, and that discourages the development of qualities that are contrary to their type.

By holding to the view that personality is a story, the coach can use personality profiles as a basis for promoting rather than limiting the process of story-making. The continual questioning of what about personality is fixed and what is changeable enables the coach and the manager to examine the past, the present and the future with a balanced sense of realism and possibility.

CASE STUDY

Catherine

Catherine had learned early on in her career that her Jungian type (according to the Myers-Briggs Type Indicator) was ISTJ (Introversion, Sensing, Thinking, Judging) – a fairly common profile for those working in auditing, accounting and other fields requiring objective analysis and an eye for detail. This fitted with her early experience of excelling in numeracy, going on to study mathematics and economics at university, training as an accountant, and then following a career in financial services. It seemed to her coach that Catherine's self-identity was strongly linked to her head for numbers.

However, discussion revealed Catherine's passion for developing her team, for organising group social events, and for encouraging her organisation to develop more people-friendly policies regarding part-time working and teleworking. The striking thing about these motivations was that they did not seem to be consistent with Catherine's personality type. Her outgoing approach to her team, and to organising social activities, suggested a fair degree of extroversion rather than introversion. Furthermore, her interest in the development of people-friendly policies indicated some preference for 'feeling' rather than 'thinking' in her decision-making.

Exploring Catherine's history it became apparent that she had been strongly encouraged to develop her practical and logical skills from an early age. Her father taught mathematics in further education and attributed particular value to Catherine's capacity to make quiet, logical, systematic judgements. She had worked hard in those subjects that required these skills and received recognition when her efforts yielded good results. Whatever 'natural' aptitude that Catherine had for objective analysis had been consistently 'nurtured' in her early years, and then reinforced in her successive roles.

In developing the personality story, her coach challenged Catherine's self-limiting identity, inviting her to explore how her analytical skills could be used in more extrovert and people-focused ways. As the coach explored new possibilities she ignited Catherine's belief that she could rediscover the enthusiasm she had for work earlier on in her career. This enthusiasm was generated by opening Catherine up to new possibilities, to a new personality story, which combined her intrinsic strengths with new challenges that she felt motivated to achieve for herself and her organisation.

THE RELATIONSHIP STORY

Constructing a story in terms of relationships can be a particularly useful perspective because relationships encapsulate many important elements of change that are considered within the ACE FIRST framework. We can consider five facets of relationships that contribute to this story.

First, there are the manager's present relationships. Whether a manager's developmental goal is to motivate others, to influence others, to consult more effectively, or to display greater confidence and assertiveness, the enactment of change will ultimately be tested in relationship with others. The way managers behave, think and feel about current work relationships provides an initial construction of the present relationship story.

Second, understanding the goals and intentions of managers in the context of their work relationships paints a picture of a desired future state for relationships, and therefore an indication of the developmental challenge for coaching.

The third facet of relationships concerns the impact of history, and the way in which early relationships and attachment patterns influence the way managers relate in the present. In this respect the relationship story contains elements of the history story.

Fourth, the relationship between managers and their coach can be viewed as a microcosm of all their relationships, recapitulating in the transference and countertransference the unconscious factors that underpin the relationship story.

Fifth – and ultimately the most important in terms of change – is the way managers relate to themselves. This can be thought of as the relationship between 'I' and 'me', which is the basis for a person's self-concept and his or her capacity to believe that he or she can change.

Bringing together information about these five facets of relationships enables the coach to construct a profound story about the coaching challenge and the factors that enable change to be realised. At this point I wish to introduce a model of relationship development that brings together these multiple elements of relationship.

Table 14 | Four purposes of a relationship

Results	The relationship is a means to an end. It is concerned with agreeing goals with another person, managing expectations and checking whether goals have been achieved.
Intimacy	The relationship is concerned with support, closeness and connection. It is characterised by the desire for, and/or demonstration of, attunement and responsiveness with another person.
Autonomy	The relationship is concerned with individuality and independence. It is characterised by an emphasis on difference and separation, and the desire to be in control within a relationship.
Trust	The relationship is concerned with commitment. It is characterised by a sense of resilience and reliability, in which intimacy and autonomy provide the basis for interdependence and personal creativity.

A model of relationship development

The model of relationships presented here is a conceptual simplification of a model arising out of research into what makes work relationships effective (Loftus, 2000; Lee, 2001).[3] We can distinguish four purposes of a relationship (see Table 14):

- to produce results
- to develop intimacy

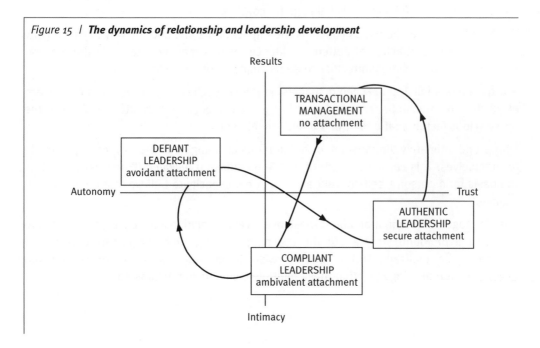

Figure 15 | The dynamics of relationship and leadership development

- to develop autonomy

- to develop trust.

Our research has demonstrated that these four purposes can be viewed as independent dimensions which can be expressed in relation to each other. Thus a relationship that is primarily focused on results will be least focused on intimacy. Similarly, a relationship that is focused on autonomy will be least focused on trust. Conceptually, we can draw these dimensions as two axes to represent a relationship space, on which at a particular moment a person's perception of his or her relationship with another person can be mapped as a point in this space. If this perception is mapped over time, we have the basis for a relationship story.

One of the most important aspects of this model is that it does not seek to provide a static account of relationships, but rather a picture of the way in which productive relationships change over time. We can envisage the ideal development of a relationship as following a figure of eight within this relationship space (see Figure 15).

Typically, a new relationship begins in the top right-hand quadrant. The purpose of the relationship is to achieve a result, but there is also a degree of provisional trust as a basis for building rapport in the relationship. As the relationship develops, the purpose is increasingly about developing 'intimacy', a sense of genuine care and concern for the other person, quite apart from the specific goals we may wish to achieve through this relationship. The move towards intimacy proceeds with a continuing provisional trust and so remains on the right-hand side of the relationship space.

As the relationship develops further there is a need to assert one's individuality and sense of difference, and this move towards 'autonomy' also brings a judgement about the degree to which the relationship is achieving desired results – thereby moving towards the top left-hand quadrant. If the sense of autonomy and difference can be negotiated, grounded in the experience of managing expectations and establishing a degree of intimacy, then the relationship can move towards trust – the basis for resilience in the relationship that encourages both interdependence and personal creativity.

Having arrived at trust, the development of the relationship does not stop. If it does, it is likely to become stale and unproductive. In a productively alive relationship the cycle is completed when new challenges and results are identified for the relationship, and the process begins again.

Relationship and leadership development

In developing the relationship story the aim is to understand managers' characteristic patterns of relating. Although it is usual for different relationships to have different qualities – some more results-focused, some more intimate, some more autonomous and some more trusting – it is often possible to discern biases that become the focus for coaching conversations. The value of this model is that it provides a framework for making sense of managers' relationships, and for understanding the development challenge in moving relationships through to the next stage. Furthermore, these relationship stages

Table 15 | *Leadership and relationship style*

Leadership style	Characteristics of relationship style	Development focus
Transactional management (Results)	Results-focused Businesslike, pragmatic Performance-management biased Uncomfortable with emotions	Aim to understand impact on others Explore why emotions are avoided Develop capacity to motivate and value others
Compliant leadership (Intimacy)	Is caring and thoughtful Is energised by recognition Needs reassurance Is responsive but potentially timid	Develop willingness to confront differences Cultivate assertiveness in balance to responsiveness Learn to provide structure and direction
Defiant leadership (Autonomy)	Independent and productive Controlling leadership with uncompromising drive Concerned about failure/rejection	Develop capacity to express feelings as well as logic Cultivate appreciation of others Aim to loosen the rigidity of style
Authentic leadership (Trust)	Handles others flexibly Invites collaboration/openness Is firm but fair in leadership Provides support and pressure	Identify energising goals Ensure that expectations are renewed to maintain energy Develop capacity to coach others

can be linked to the different styles of leadership that I distinguished in Chapter 1 – that is, compliant, defiant and authentic leadership (see Table 15) – as well as to patterns of attachment based on early relationships with parents (as discussed in Chapter 3).

Transactional management is not characterised by a focus on relationships, but is primarily results-focused. Although this may represent an early stage in relationships, it is quite common to find managers stuck at this style. They describe their relationships in pragmatic terms and do not expect to cultivate a meaningful interpersonal connection with others at work. In my experience this approach to relationships is based on a stark division between home and work. Home is viewed as the place for interpersonal connection, and work as the place for getting things done. I have come across this most commonly in finance or technology departments. The developmental challenge is to encourage these managers to consider the benefits of engaging more fully with others by cultivating intimacy.

In compliant leadership managers are caring and thoughtful, and they have a strong desire for recognition. They can be timid and need to develop their capacity for autonomy, which entails being more assertive and being prepared to confront differences.

In defiant leadership managers are independent and controlling, and can be critical of others. Although their uncompromising drive can get things done, they tend to evoke resistance and frustration in others. Their development challenge is to be more open to their feelings and those of others, and to find ways of relating that inspire rather than coerce.

In authentic leadership managers are flexible, matching their style to different people and circumstances, and offering a balance between pressure and support. Their development challenge is to sustain energy in their relationships by setting new goals and explicitly renegotiating expectations. Crucially, authentic leadership can only be arrived at through working through the transactional, compliant and defiant aspects of the relationship cycle.

CASE STUDY

Gordon, *continued*

A key challenge for Gordon was to develop his ability to handle confrontational meetings more effectively by stepping in to facilitate productive discussions. In working with Gordon I constructed a relationship story that also included an understanding of how his present relationships were influenced by his earliest relationships, particularly that with this father.

I knew from his boss that Gordon needed to show more influence and personal impact in difficult senior meetings. In describing many of his work relationships it was apparent that Gordon wanted them to be harmonious, and he would appease others. This appeasing side was also evident in the transference, where he would tend to agree with me rather too readily, and I could find myself (in my countertransference) feeling frustrated by the formality of our conversations.

In terms of the relationship model described above, I thought Gordon showed a bias towards compliant leadership, evidenced by his desire for harmony and his fear of confrontation with senior colleagues. However, this was not the whole story. The compliant side of Gordon was compensated for by a more authentic leadership style in relation to his own team members. If disagreement arose in his own team, he seemed to handle the issues effectively, allowing different parties to voice their feelings and encouraging people to listen to each other. But he did not personally attribute much value to his leadership competence with his own team, and so his relationship with himself regarding his handling of conflict was a strongly self-critical one. He noticed his failures and ignored his successes.

Bringing the historical dimension to bear on this relationship story, I noted that Gordon, as the eldest son, was expected by his father to set an example to his brother, two years his junior. If they did get into a fight or argument, his father would withdraw in silent disgust, evoking a powerful sense of rejection and failure in Gordon. In many circumstances Gordon showed great maturity with his brother, and it seemed to me that this paralleled his effective handling of relationships in his own team. However, Gordon was unable to express his frustration at his father's disapproving withdrawal. He had felt ashamed and rejected, and had learned to hide his own feelings.

My hypothesis was that, based on his early experiences of his father's disapproval, Gordon had repressed his own anger in order to present a pleasing façade. In the present-day circumstances of confrontational meetings Gordon was repeating a pattern of withdrawal learned since childhood. I thought that Gordon was unconsciously fearful that his own anger would be triggered, and that if it was expressed he would lose the respect of his colleagues, just as he felt he had done with his father.

Summary

Story-making is the stage at which the coach constructs hypotheses about the developmental challenges facing managers. The concept of 'story' emphasises that these hypotheses are not essential truths, but constructions that ought to be useful for facilitating change. Making a story, the coach is encouraged to entertain multiple perspectives and to view the story as emerging out of the dialogue between coach and manager. The ACE FIRST model of change encourages coaches to consider alternative stories because it invites them to collect information from multiple perspectives. I have considered five possible stories that can be constructed using different elements of the ACE FIRST model – that is: the systemic story, the cognitive story, the history story, the personality story and the relationship story.

ENDNOTES

1   The concept of story-making derives from narrative therapy (White and Epston, 1990), which is itself underpinned by the concept of social constructionism (Gergen, 1985). According to social constructionism, ideas, practices and beliefs arise not through the discovery of objective realities, but through social interaction over time. This view of reality can be described as intersubjective in the sense that a person's reality is constructed in the space between two subjectivities: self and others.

2   Much of the current research into temperament – the aspect of personality that is defined by genetic inheritance – is focused on the so-called 'big five' factors (Digman, 1990; Ewen, 1998). Four of these factors are included in Jungian type indicators: social adaptability (extroversion-introversion), openness (intuiting-sensing), agreeableness (thinking-feeling) and conscientiousness (judging-perceiving). The fifth factor is emotional stability, and refers to the degree to which a person shows a tendency towards low anxiety and steadiness, or towards volatility and high anxiety.

3   The relationship development model developed by OCG Limited identifies six independent dimensions of relationships: transactional, intense, difficult, lacking, trusting and energising. For the purpose of using this model to help in constructing a relationship story for leadership coaching I have focused on just four dimensions of relationships: getting results (transactional), intimacy (intense), autonomy (difficult, lacking) and trust. Many management development practitioners use the online psychometric *the Relationship Q* for measuring and developing the effectiveness of relationships. This tool is particularly useful for building the relationship story in coaching. More information about the Relationship Q is available at www.ocg.co.uk.

7
Enabling

It is one thing to show a man he is in error, and another to put him in possession of the truth.

John Locke (1632–1704)

Enabling is the fourth stage in the LASER coaching process. At this stage the coach reflects on possible interventions for promoting change. Drawing on the insights gained through the earlier stages of *assessing* and *story-making* the coach weighs up possibilities, making predictions about which interventions will be enabling and which are more likely to be limiting. This process of prediction is undertaken as a piece of silent reflection on the part of the coach (or sometimes as collaborative reflection in supervision). Based on judgements about which story most usefully captures the manager's development challenges, the coach identifies specific interventions that are most likely to evoke sustainable change.

The importance of this stage should not be underestimated. In my experience coaches often leap upon the first intervention that comes to mind, eager to be useful to the manager and to demonstrate their expertise. Although such interventions may be intuitively sound, their usefulness to the manager depends on their timing and the way in which they are delivered. A premature intervention proposed in the wrong way can limit change by evoking the manager's defences. If the conscious and unconscious emotional agenda associated with these defences is understood, then the manager can make interventions that take account of these emotions.

CASE STUDY

Mark

Sensing Mark's current dissatisfaction with the company he had worked with for his entire career, his coach commented: 'I think you are not sure if this company is the right place for you. Perhaps you need to think about your career options. When did you last update your CV?'

Mark replied that he had not updated his CV for more than a decade, and that it would probably be a good idea to do that. They agreed that they would work on Mark's CV together in the next session. However, Mark cancelled the following session, and when he did meet with his coach he said that although he was under pressure, he felt he was coping fine.

The coach sensed that Mark was backing-off from the idea of exploring his career options.

In discussion with him about this session I asked the coach to describe his impression of the development challenge facing Mark. The coach outlined how Mark was allowing himself to be imprisoned by the demands of the company. Mark needed to recognise that he could influence his role, and that he could make a choice about whether the role suited him. The coach's intuitive intervention was to challenge what he believed was Mark's self-limiting belief. The intervention had failed in that it evoked Mark's defences, discouraging rather than facilitating his capacity to change. Furthermore, from the organisation's point of view it was counterproductive because they wanted to keep and develop Mark.

In my view the coach's construction of the development challenge for Mark was potentially useful, but its usefulness depended on the coach taking time to reflect on how to use his insight. Mark did need to feel he had choices and to be more empowered. But he needed his coach to acknowledge, understand and work with his emotional agenda – his fear of change. Without such acknowledgement Mark was unlikely to consider his wider options.

In this chapter I begin by considering the change cycle as a model for illustrating the fundamental importance of working with emotions at the *enabling* stage. Then I consider each of the five stories discussed in the previous chapter – the systemic story, the cognitive story, the history story, the personality story and the relationship story – and outline key interventions that are enabling or limiting in the context of each of these stories. Finally, I consider the kinds of approach that are most likely to be enabling according to whether the leadership style is authentic, defiant or compliant.

THE CHANGE CYCLE

There is a pattern of feelings that people typically go through when they experience change, whether that change is personal, interpersonal or organisational. This pattern is illustrated by the change cycle as shown in Figure 16. In practice, there are many subtleties that are not captured by this model, but the framework is useful for characterising common features of change and for thinking about the need to understand and acknowledge emotions in coaching.

The vertical axis represents a person's emotional state, ranging from positive feelings to difficult feelings. The horizontal axis represents time. Individuals vary in their experience of change, and so the time and amplitude of this cycle will depend on the individual and his or her circumstances.

To illustrate the stages of the change cycle consider someone – a woman, say – who takes on a new job. When she first takes on the job she feels optimistic, but this

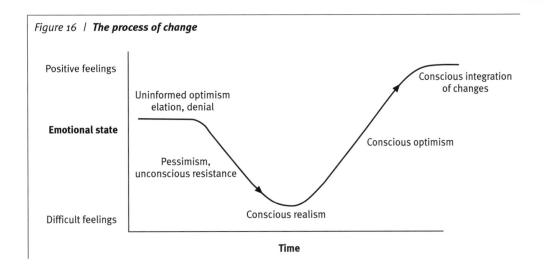

*Figure 16 | **The process of change***

optimism is based on relatively little information about the job – we can therefore describe this stage as that of uninformed optimism. Even if the change is unwanted, such as being made redundant, an individual's feelings still follow this change cycle. At this first stage she is protected from the full force of difficult feelings due to shock or unconscious denial.

At the next stage in the process, when the person has been in the new job long enough to realise that the role has its inevitable problems, there are feelings of pessimism and disillusionment, and there may be unconscious resistance to change. At this stage she is feeling less positive than at the outset, but the unconscious aspects of the experience means that she is still protected from the full reality of the change. It is at the next stage, when she has a conscious and realistic understanding of the challenges of her new role that she feels at her worst. She no longer idealises the possibilities of the role, but has a down-to-earth understanding of what she must do to achieve new goals.

It is with this conscious appreciation of the task of change that the person becomes consciously optimistic, trying out new solutions in her role and feeling more positive. Finally, she feels most positive when she has integrated her understanding of the change, and she knows how she can achieve her goals.

This model is generally useful for helping people to understand where they are in the process of change. For example, I was asked to provide support for a group of employees in New York who witnessed, live, the second plane fly into the twin towers of the World Trade Center. I used this model to help them to understand their mix of emotions as they came to terms with the trauma – in particular normalising their experiences of fear and powerlessness – and its impact on their capacity to concentrate and function normally. As they gained more information about the realities of what had happened, and became more conscious of their emotional responses to fear, they gradually became more optimistic about the future, and could focus again on the normal aspects of their lives.

Understanding and acknowledging emotions

Applying this model to coaching we can envisage the process of change following a path similar to that described by the change cycle. At the outset many managers will be positive and optimistic about the opportunity to develop themselves and will be feeling good. However, as they look more closely at themselves and receive feedback from colleagues, their feelings are likely to become more mixed, and they will show some unconscious resistance to change. Other managers who, from the outset, are resistant to the process of coaching may enter coaching at the pessimistic stage of the change cycle. They are defended against their potential to change, and embark on coaching grudgingly as a result of external pressure.

At this enabling stage of coaching we are concerned with understanding how to shift managers from the left-hand slope of the change cycle, in order to move them through conscious realism, towards the upward slope of optimism and the integration of new changes. To do this the coach considers two separate sets of interventions.

The first is concerned with acknowledging conscious and unconscious emotions surrounding the possibility of change. If emotions are made conscious and are acknowledged, managers can move through the change cycle.

Acknowledgement and understanding allows them to be open to the second set of interventions – those concerned with identifying options and solutions, and with planning actions to realise change (see Figure 17).

It is always tempting for coaches to move too quickly to the second set of interventions, recommending solutions and prescribing actions. However, if the emotions associated

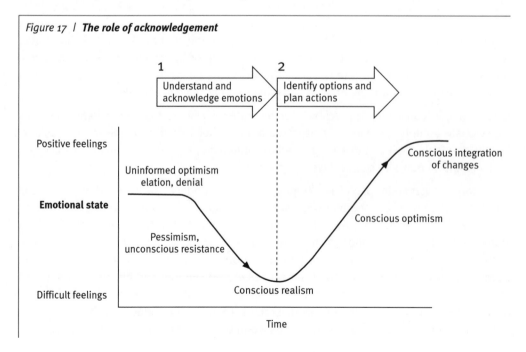

Figure 17 / **The role of acknowledgement**

with unconscious resistance to change have not been addressed, such interventions will fail. Even if managers agree to adopt new behaviours, and consciously intend to follow through on their commitment to change, subsequent evaluation shows that these managers usually revert to their former style of behaviour.

CASE STUDY

Mark, *continued*

As described at the beginning of this chapter, Mark's coach quickly identified options and actions for change – for Mark to work on his CV and to explore new career opportunities. The coach's intention was to evoke Mark's sense of empowerment. However, Mark's defensiveness demonstrated that the coach's intervention was ill-timed. Mark was not ready to move to the stage of conscious optimism about the possibilities in his career because his emotional agenda had not been adequately addressed.

In reflecting about what had happened the coach realised that he had become frustrated with Mark's apparent self-sufficiency. Although Mark was obviously under a great deal of stress, he portrayed his role as stimulating rather than draining, and any dissatisfaction with his role as resulting from temporary staff shortages. What the coach had previously failed to realise was that Mark's self-sufficiency was a façade designed to hide his fear of rejection. Reminding himself of the history story and the fact that Mark had been sent to boarding school from an early age, the coach realised that Mark's façade was a powerful coping mechanism that disguised a shaky self-confidence. He had learned to comply during his years at boarding school, and he had applied that learning to his work roles ever since.

The coach realised that he needed to shift his focus to the earlier stage in the change cycle – he needed to make interventions that acknowledged the emotional issues underpinning Mark's resistance. The coach decided to explore Mark's experiences of boarding school in more detail and their relevance to Mark's coping strategies at work. Further, examining his countertransference reaction to Mark (ie pushing Mark to take action), the coach realised that his brusque, no-nonsense approach was an unconscious repetition of Mark's experience of his teachers at boarding school. The coach hypothesised that if he was able to provide more empathy and concern for Mark's emotions, Mark might allow his defences to relax.

This process of reflection about what would be enabling for Mark achieved its intended result. Mark quickly responded to his coach's more empathic style, and talked briefly about how frightened he had been at boarding school. Although an artistic and imaginative boy, he had quickly learned to present himself as tough and task-focused in order to divert potential bullying.

These insights led to a discussion of Mark's boss, and the degree to which Mark allowed himself to be overburdened with work. After taking time to explore the emotional impact of these experiences and their link to his present circumstances, Mark was then ready to consider options and actions that would enable him to undertake useful and sustainable change. With the grounding of increased awareness, and the acknowledgement of his emotions, Mark had been enabled to move towards real change.

USING STORIES TO ENABLE CHANGE

In the previous chapter I described five stories that are useful for making sense of the process of change for managers – the systemic, cognitive, history, personality and relationship stories. From the perspective of each of these stories there are certain interventions that coaches can make that are likely to be enabling, and others that are likely to be limiting. I examine each of these stories and highlight a number of factors that must be considered to ensure that interventions at the reframing stage are enabling.

The systemic story

The great value of the systemic story is that it encourages coaches to take account of the complexity of the context in which managers are operating. The focus is to some extent shifted away from individual psychology towards interpersonal, organisational and cultural issues. This perspective brings realism to managers' expectations of the degree of change achievable, since some of the factors influencing their capacity to change lie outside their sphere of influence (Covey, 1989).

For example, a marketing manager was frustrated by the lack of co-operation he was receiving from his research colleagues. The systemic story showed that the problem lay to a large extent with the animosity between the marketing director and the research director, and this lack of co-operation filtered down into other relationships between the departments. In seeking to improve relationships with his research colleagues, the relationship between the senior directors was outside the marketing manager's sphere of influence. He could not *make* them have a better relationship.

In working with the systemic story, coaches have to strike a balance between acknowledging wider concerns while aiming to shift the focus of conversation towards the manager's sphere of influence. If a manager is allowed to dwell on issues that are outside his or her sphere of influence, the coach is supporting a mindset of powerlessness, and the potential for the manager to change is limited. On the other hand, if the coach focuses exclusively on a manager's personal development, ignoring how possibilities are constrained by the system, unrealistic expectations will limit the potential for change. Having acknowledged feelings about systemic issues, the coach identifies specific skills and actions that will enable the manager to exert a positive influence on his or her organisational context.

In the case of the marketing manager, although he could not directly influence the relationship between the research director and the marketing director, he could take a number of actions to cultivate more productive relationships with his direct contacts within the research department.

The cognitive story

The cognitive story describes the patterns of thinking that underpin a manager's behaviour, and when used effectively to inform the coach's interventions it can yield dramatic change. For example, managers encouraged to 'check out' their impact on colleagues, rather than using 'mind reading' to assume the worst, may be surprised to discover that they are highly regarded, and this can readily promote an intention to seek feedback more actively in the future.

In working with the cognitive story, coaches must be active in identifying enabling and limiting cognitions (see Table 13, page 99) and in deciding how to work with them. The overarching aim is to reinforce enabling beliefs and to examine or challenge limiting beliefs. If a manager repeatedly demonstrates the use of limiting cognitions and the coach neither explores the basis for these attitudes nor challenges their validity, then the attitude will be inadvertently reinforced.

For example, a manager who says 'I am so disorganised and unreliable' will be reinforced in this self-appraisal if the coach either does not ask for more information about this belief, or does not challenge it with some countering information. In challenging the belief the coach might note that the manager arrived for the session on time and point out that this suggests a fair degree of organisation. In the challenge managers are invited to examine the clash between their self-belief and certain objective facts.

In probing about a particular belief the coach can take either of two paths. One is to understand the belief in terms of its implications for the manager's emotions and actions. This expansion of the conversation from a focus on cognitions to the full ACE pattern can enable change because random elements of a manager's experience are collected together into a meaningful whole.

For example, over exaggeration about setbacks (cognition) is linked with depression (emotion) and a lack of concentration on finding new solutions (action). The coherence of the ACE pattern gives managers and the coach something meaningful to work with. In contrast, a focus on the limiting cognition in isolation (eg 'This is a disaster') can lead to an unhelpful search for evidence to support the belief (eg to prove it really is a disaster).

The second path for probing about a particular attitude is to surface core beliefs that underpin it. This is particularly enabling for managers whose spontaneous thoughts are persistently limiting. For example, a manager who repeatedly demonstrates low self-esteem with negative prophecy ('I'll mess it up') and who discounts the positive ('My ideas don't make any difference') is unlikely to change by simply trying to replace his or her limiting cognitions with enabling ones, 'positive prophecy' and 'valuing the positive'. The coach will have to unpack the basis for this low self-esteem, and in particular to understand the unconscious emotional issues holding this cognition in place.

The history story

Although many coaches take a personal history during the assessing stage, it is quite common to view history-taking as an isolated activity that is not referred to again during the course of coaching. Coaches can feel as if, after assessment, they should now be focusing exclusively on present-day performance improvements, and that to refer back to history seems like a backward step. Such a view limits the value of the history story for enabling change.

In my experience it is inevitable that during the course of coaching, present-day issues will surface that raise questions in the mind of the coach about some unexplored aspect of a manager's history. To work effectively with the history story the coach must reinforce the ongoing making of links between past and present as a normal aspect of coaching conversations. Once the usefulness of these links to present performance is established, managers will more readily look for such links in subsequent conversations.

Although making links between the past and the present can be transformative, coaches must be sensitive to the emotional readiness of managers to make use of such links. A premature introduction of links is likely to produce defensiveness. Furthermore, in making links between the past and the present, managers can sometimes view their historical experiences as constraining future choices. Such a view limits a manager's sense of choice. The coach must emphasise that choices are limited while past-present links remain unconscious. When they have been brought into awareness, managers are enabled to make conscious choices about how they will behave in the future. Clarity about the value of consciousness in relation to making links encourages managers to search for greater self-awareness with positive curiosity.

The personality story

One of the main benefits of the personality story is that it can help to discern between which of the stories is most likely to be useful for managers. Individuals have different preferences over how they take in information, how they make decisions, and how they learn. An awareness of these preferences from the personality story helps coaches to match their approach to individual preferences.

For example, consider a manager who is practical and detailed, and who has a strong need to see how coaching conversations will be immediately useful in his or her role. (In terms of the Myers-Briggs Type Indicator this manager might be ISTJ – introvert, sensing, thinking, judging.) For such a manager it will be useful to use the systemic story and the cognitive story. The systemic story will demonstrate the coach's understanding of the manager's working context and the way in which coaching conversations can grapple with the practical realities of business life. The cognitive story will provide the manager with a method for self-reflection that is grounded in objective observations about the use of language and its implications for thoughts, feelings and behaviours. These stories are the ones most congruent with the manager's own personality preferences, and can be reinforced by discussions about detailed action plans, with timelines for measuring results.

In contrast, consider a manager who is more open-ended and who enjoys playing with ideas and possibilities. He or she learns less by focusing on measurable goals and more by understanding ideas in terms of their impact on people, and by trying out new activities. (In terms of the Myers-Briggs Type Indicator this manager might be ENFP – extrovert, intuitive, feeling, perceiving.) For such a manager it will be useful to use the history story and the relationship story. The history story will appeal to his or her interest in making links and finding patterns. The relationship story will appeal to his or her need to understand the interpersonal dimension and the way in which his or her behaviour impacts on others. Building on the relationship story, this manager is likely to welcome the opportunity to plan specific conversations with a view to developing certain key relationships.

As well as helping to distinguish between the usefulness of different stories, the personality story also provides a source of specific information about managers' strengths and potential development areas. To enable effective change, coaches have to balance the reinforcement of strengths, the working with development areas, and the acceptance and management of limitations. However, coaches must be cautious about the potential for managers to view their strengths and weaknesses as fixed and prescribed by their personality profile, thereby supporting the status quo rather than a drive for change.

The relationship story

One of the most enabling aspects of the relationship story is its potential to normalise managers' varied experiences of relationships. Managers are often confused by why certain relationships are problematic whereas others are more easily effective, and they tend either to blame themselves or the other person for difficulties. In contrast to this either/or perspective, the relationship story encourages them to view the experience of the relationship as arising out of the interaction of two people, just as the outputs of coaching arise out of the interactions between coach and manager. Furthermore, the relationship story places their experience within a normal process of relationship development. If their feelings are stuck, they can see that identifying actions to shift the relationship is a useful focus for coaching. In contrast, if managers are encouraged to view relationship difficulties as an insoluble problem, indicative of some fundamental incompatibility between themselves and a colleague, then their potential for change will be limited.

A further enabling aspect of the relationship story is that it highlights that managers have a choice over which relationships to cultivate. By being explicit about the purpose of relationships for achieving personal and organisational goals, managers recognise that they do not have to develop all relationships to be effective. Different needs may be achieved through different relationships, and tailoring efforts appropriately to different relationships supports a more manageable attitude to relationship development.

An examination of present relationships can be viewed as a means-to-an-end process, in which the manager targets new behaviours towards specific individuals to achieve specific results. Although this process has potential value, it can be limiting if coaching discussions are not broadened in order to develop the manager's self-awareness. This broadening involves looking at the emotional issues that are evoked by different relationships, looking for patterns of relating that seem to predominate and, possibly, exploring how these patterns have been formed through early experiences. Through this process of exploration, the present-day relationship story is linked to the history story, thereby enabling a greater depth of self-knowledge and a greater potential to express authenticity.

ENABLING CHANGE ACCORDING TO LEADERSHIP STYLE

The identification of a manager's predominant leadership style (authentic, compliant or defiant) provides a further basis for identifying interventions that will be enabling. This perspective brings together constructions about the likely unconscious factors underpinning the leadership style, and encourages the development of authentic leadership.

Below, I consider those factors that are likely to be enabling or limiting according to each of the three styles.

Authentic leadership

Managers who demonstrate authentic leadership are relatively open to change. They welcome the opportunity to make use of the learning space provided by coaching, and need a coach who is prepared to offer a flexible mix of structure and empathy. The coach's aim is to evoke the creativity of managers, to help them to set stretching goals for themselves, and to energise them to achieve results that are personally and organisationally rewarding. In terms of the change cycle discussed above, these managers are quickly ready to consider new possibilities (conscious optimism) and find coaching most useful when they are challenged to shape their goals into precise and measurable action plans. Often the biggest block to their capacity to change is the high demands on their time, and clarifying specific actions helps to establish explicit priorities.

There are a number of interventions that coaches can make that are limiting for these managers. If the coach is too directive or if the coach places too much emphasis on feelings about change, managers will not be able to use the relationship productively. For example, coaches working with successful managers may sometimes probe for emotional issues because they feel that they can only be of use to managers if they can identify emotional problems to solve. On the other hand, coaches can fail to see the value of exerting pressure around specific goals because they think that managers are competent to make things happen. The challenge of enabling change in managers who display authentic leadership is to provide a role model of supportive empowerment, striking a balance between structure and empathy.

Compliant leadership

As noted in relation to the change cycle, these managers do not engage with fundamental change if the coach does not address their emotional resistance. They need their coach to provide emotional resilience and structure, since it is their experience of the coach as robust that enables them to know and express their unconscious frustrations underlying their compliant style. If the coach is too appeasing or excessively empathic, these managers tend to dwell on issues that are outside their control, reinforcing a deeper sense of disempowerment and a need to comply to maintain some sense of security.

The coach must acknowledge their emotions and reinforce their strengths, since these managers often minimise their successes while overemphasising their apparent failures. Only once emotions have been understood and acknowledged will these managers be in a position to think freshly about their goals and aspirations. Furthermore, it is important that the coach allows goals to be generated by these managers, despite the temptation to provide direction for them. If the coach does drive the identification of goals, there is a danger that these managers will comply, but will not have engaged their authentic desire for change.

CASE STUDY

Gordon, *continued*

In developing Gordon's capacity for authentic leadership I thought that I needed to work with his fear of confrontation – something that was very apparent in meetings when tensions were running high. I decided that I needed to acknowledge his unconscious frustration at feeling as if he had to comply in order to be accepted by others. He did not believe that he could be selfish or emotional and at the same time be liked by others. He unconsciously assumed that he would receive disapproval in the way he had perceived disapproval from his father.

I decided that the most enabling approach for Gordon would be to begin by reinforcing his current areas of strength – in particular, his effective handling of confrontation with members of his own team. Starting in this way would help to establish the learning space as constructive and supportive, and would challenge him to value his own sense of competence. Then I would make links between his experience of his father and his experience of senior colleagues during difficult meetings, and show how he was projecting his earlier experience into the present. The purpose of making these links would be to bring Gordon's unconscious frustrations to the surface, and my aim would be to provide space to reflect on these feelings without being excessively sympathetic. I thought that my sympathy would tend to discourage his capacity to experiment with expressing frustration.

Finally, I considered the possibility of working with Gordon's cognitive story. One of his core beliefs was that showing frustration or anger lacked integrity (one of his father's rules). I thought that we might need to explore examples of behaviours that were authentic precisely because they did encompass genuine feelings, even if those feelings were of frustration and anger.

These interventions were intended to enable change by acknowledging Gordon's emotions. With such acknowledgement I hypothesised that Gordon would readily identify actions for change.

This case study is continued in the next chapter.

Defiant leadership

Unlike the manager whose bias is towards compliant leadership, these managers have unconsciously learned to manage their emotions by holding others at a distance, by exerting control, and by tackling issues with logic. If coaches seek to structure these managers or to intellectualise issues, they are likely to evoke competitiveness, and a competitive learning space is not one that is likely to nurture the surfacing of feelings. To enable these managers to change, coaches must provide empathy, understanding and reflection. The coaching space has to be one in which managers have an opportunity for *being* rather than *doing* (see Chapter 4), and in which coaches persistently invite them to explore their feelings rather than practical solutions.

In my experience these managers tend to test the emotional resilience of the coach early in the relationship, and if the coach does not meet this challenge in the right way, the coaching relationship is undermined. The challenge may take the form of questioning the professional expertise of the coach, or of trying to change the venue, length or number of coaching sessions. It is essential that coaches understand this challenge as part of a repertoire of defence – to control rather than to expose themselves to scrutiny. Although coaches must be prepared to establish their professional credibility or to explore the parameters of the coaching contract, this should usually have occurred during the initial establishment of the learning space.

Usually it is more enabling to turn the discussion around and to explore the feelings that these managers have about what will happen during coaching. Thus from the outset the coach seeks to meet defiance with a firm but compassionate curiosity about feelings. I should note that this sounds simple to do, but in practice a challenging and defiant senior manager can easily evoke defensiveness in the coach, just as such a manager does with his or her colleagues. It is at these moments that the coach's capacity to understand the transference and countertransference is essential.

If coaches can meet these challenges, they can begin to bring the managers' feelings of vulnerability to the surface so that failures, setbacks or shortcomings can be acknowledged in a non-judgemental way. The aim is to discourage habitual patterns of projecting feelings of imperfection or inadequacy, and to explore their feelings about being good enough.

CASE STUDY

Elizabeth, *continued*

At the outset of my work with Elizabeth she had challenged the idea that she needed coaching, despite her boss's encouragement. She knew that she was being considered for a senior management position, but that her boss was concerned about her barbed relationship with a number of colleagues. In our first session she had challenged the idea that she would be able to attend a series of coaching sessions (see Chapter 4, page 64), but had changed her mind when she found that I met her challenge with a firm statement that we should not agree to regular sessions at this stage. I had engaged her interest by paradoxically not seeking to control her.

After two sessions Elizabeth had provided an outline of her personal development goals and a sketch of her personal history. She did not want to talk about her background, but she did tell me that her mother had often been depressed and drank heavily. Her father was a very successful academic whom she loved, but who had often been away travelling.

Having touched on this historical perspective, Elizabeth wanted to get on with thinking about how she could get promoted. In response to this I had suggested that we look at some 360-degree feedback from her boss and colleagues to identify the most useful areas for development. The feedback was strongly critical and Elizabeth became very defensive. She said that her colleagues were incompetent and accused them of being envious of her. And then, at the end of this session, she raised doubt about whether she could come to the next coaching session.

Elizabeth was showing a resistance to feedback and to making links, and she was beginning to turn her defensiveness onto me. I had to think about what I could do to enable Elizabeth to engage more deeply with the process of change. I decided that my first priority was to address her sense that I had failed her by giving credence to the critical 360-degree feedback. I needed to empathise with her feelings. I imagined saying to her, 'Whether the criticism is fair or not, I know that I would find it very painful to find out that my colleagues perceived me that way. It is understandable that you feel indignant, but I think you must also feel very hurt.'

To further reinforce the validity of her feelings I also decided to talk to her about the need to understand how she had experienced feedback in the past, in particular from her mother and father. My impression was that her alcoholic mother could be fiercely rejecting, and it was in that relationship that Elizabeth's defiant (avoidant) attachment pattern had been formed. If I could encourage Elizabeth to look more closely at these earlier experiences, I thought that we would be able to make a useful link to her current sense of rejection by her colleagues.

This case study is continued in the next chapter.

Summary

At the enabling stage the coach reflects on possible interventions to facilitate change, and distinguishes those that will be enabling from those that will be limiting. The change cycle illustrates that in making interventions, understanding and acknowledging emotions must precede the identification of solutions and action plans. Without acknowledging emotions, managers' resistance to change will be reinforced. With acknowledgement, managers' defences will relax and they will be more open to new possibilities.

Turning to the five types of story – the systemic, cognitive, history, personality and relationship stories – specific interventions are highlighted that are likely to be enabling or limiting when used in the reframing stage. An understanding of the emotional agenda underpinning each leadership style also indicates specific interventions that are likely to be enabling or limiting.

8

Reframing

The real act of discovery consists not in finding new lands but seeing with new eyes.

Marcel Proust (1871–1922)

Reframing is the fifth and final stage in the Laser coaching process. It is during this stage that the coach makes interventions that promote change. The term 'framing' refers to how people see and make sense of experiences – the frame they put around their view of themselves and others. A fixed frame is an unchanging way of interpreting events and is part of the stability and continuity of self-identity. Frames hold together established ACE FIRST patterns and can resist new possibilities for change. 'Re-framing' refers to a shift in perspective – a new way of seeing and experiencing that takes in new possibilities and that opens the door to change.

For example, a manager who views meetings as a bureaucratic bore will approach them with apathy or frustration. But if the manager reframes meetings as an opportunity for creativity, for building relationships, for experimenting with influence skills, then new ways of feeling, thinking and behaving will be triggered.

Reframing facilitates change by providing new points of view. The approach to coaching presented in this book emphasises the benefit of focusing on multiple perspectives, and so readily provides options for reframing. Selecting between these options, or at least deciding the sequence for a series of interventions, is constructed and evaluated during

---

Figure 18 | Reframing changes viewing and doing

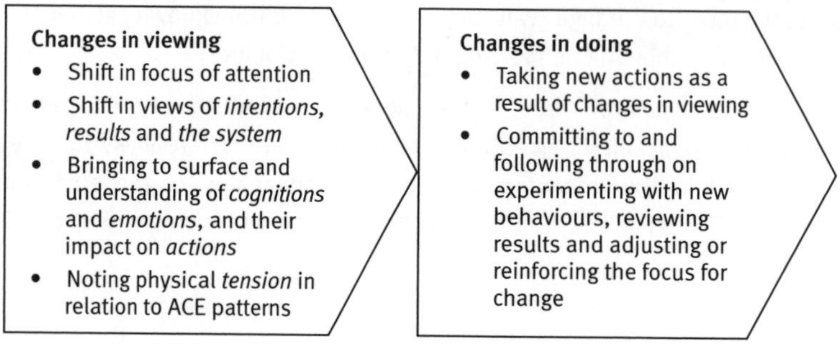

Changes in viewing
- Shift in focus of attention
- Shift in views of *intentions, results* and *the system*
- Bringing to surface and understanding of *cognitions* and *emotions*, and their impact on *actions*
- Noting physical *tension* in relation to ACE patterns

Changes in doing
- Taking new actions as a result of changes in viewing
- Committing to and following through on experimenting with new behaviours, reviewing results and adjusting or reinforcing the focus for change

the *story-making* and *enabling* stages of the coaching process. At the reframing stage, specific interventions are used to evoke change, whether that change is in terms of self-awareness, understanding others, or taking specific actions to achieve agreed goals. In this sense I am using 'reframing' as an umbrella term to cover all the interventions that a coach can make to enable change, whether the interventions evoke a change in 'viewing' or a change in 'doing' (see Figure 18).

Changes in *viewing* are concerned with shifting focus to different elements of an ACE FIRST pattern, bringing unconscious factors to the surface, and making links in order to identify predominant patterns. These changes in viewing are the basis for self-awareness and personal insight. Changes in *doing* are concerned with enabling managers to adopt new actions as a result of their increased awareness. These actions usually take the form of identifying experiments for making changes, and in subsequent sessions, reviewing the results of those experiments.

Below, I describe a number of specific interventions in relation to each of the primary targets for change – actions, cognitions and emotions. However, I consider them in reverse order since, as discussed in the previous chapter, it is usually the acknowledging of emotions and cognitions that paves the way for discussions about new actions. Having said that, in practice, discussions throughout the LASER coaching process must move flexibly across all of the elements of ACE FIRST patterns, and this is no less the case at the reframing stage. I close this chapter with a consideration of 'endings' in coaching, and how managing the ending influences the degree to which insights gained through reframing are internalised as sustainable change.

REFRAMING EMOTIONS

The coach's goal in relation to emotions is to bring them to the surface, acknowledge them, and make sense of them. An acknowledged emotion changes, whereas an unacknowledged emotion stays the same, unconsciously exerting its constraining influence on possibilities.

Working with emotions has two aspects. The first is concerned with bringing emotions into consciousness, and I discuss two interventions that help to achieve this, using silence and reflecting. The second aspect is concerned with acknowledging and making sense of emotions, for which I describe three interventions – normalising, externalising and making links.

Using silence

It may seem odd to describe being silent as an intervention in coaching, and yet it is a key technique. It is within an attentive silence that managers come to know their internal emotional states and their ways of processing experiences. These moments of self-knowing are central aspects of self-awareness – what in emotional intelligence is described as 'knowing one's emotions'. Talking, theorising, comparing, judging, planning – these can be unconscious forms of defence against emotional experiencing, and it is all too easy for the coach to collude with these defences.

As a colleague used to say, 'Ask an open question, and then zip the lip.' One of the reasons that coaches can fail to 'zip the lip' is because they feel uncomfortable with the emotional tension that is created by silence. They diffuse the tension by following a question with other questions, or by suggesting options for answers to a question – for example, 'What do you feel about this feedback?', ' ... On balance do you think it is a fair reflection of your performance?', ' ... You must be pleased with this positive comment.' Such repetitive and leading questions close down the space for emotional experiencing.

This closing down to emotional knowing can occur in other ways too, such as when coaches structure sessions to maintain a practical task focus to conversations, or when they prematurely share their ideas or expertise.

The expectation that coaching is, in part, designed to provide a space for self-discovery, discussed and enacted by the coach through the creation of the learning space, sets the scene for the productive use of silence. When managers pause or come to the end of a sentence, coaches have an important moment of choice. They can ask a question, they can make a comment, they can invite a change of direction in the conversation. Or they can remain silent. Choosing to remain silent can be a powerful option for bringing emotions to the surface and eliciting self-disclosure. Silence can serve as an invitation to managers to look inwards, to introspect, to make their own links between feelings, thoughts and behaviours, and in making such links to discover their own insights.

Silence in the presence of another person evokes a kind of self-knowing that is not available within the silence of solitude. It is a self-knowing that is concerned with how a person expects to be perceived by others, informed as it is by their unconscious projections and assumptions. For many, silence is a loaded phenomenon in its own right, evoking a sense of being judged, of being criticised, of being ignored, of needing to perform, of needing to fill the silence. Surfacing and recognising these feelings provides insight into how managers experience and relate to others, and the unconscious challenges they face in expressing authenticity within a social context.

Used effectively, silence evokes the capacity of managers to reframe their experiences, encouraging them to reflect in novel ways about their emotions, and to give voice to those feelings in the presence of their coach. These moments of self-discovery – valued, shaped and reinforced through discussion with the coach – provide the basis for important insights.

Reflecting

A further technique for surfacing emotion is reflecting. In reflecting, coaches seek to show understanding in a way that is non-directive and non-evaluative, and which encourages managers to say more about their experiences. Like the use of silence, reflecting is not used to offer suggestions or insights, but rather to evoke the capacity of managers to discover their own insights.

I can distinguish reflecting from other types of response with an illustration.

Consider a manager who reports to his or her coach, 'I am very ambitious. I have done well in a number of roles, and I will make this new role a success, even if I have to ruffle some feathers along the way.' A reflecting response might be to say, 'You feel you are very ambitious.' The response is non-directive in that it does not seek to push the conversation in one direction or another. Its relative blandness encourages the manager to elaborate his or her views, minimally influenced by the views of the coach. Such non-directive responses, first described by Carl Rogers (1961, 1967), are sometimes parodied as an unthinking repeating back of what the person said. However, used at the right time such responses evoke reflection and lead managers towards their own insights.

We can contrast reflecting with a number of other responses. A *probing* response might be to ask, 'Why do you feel you need to succeed?' A *supportive* response might be to say, 'I think your positive motivation to succeed will help you to do well.' An *interpreting* response might be to say, 'It seems to me that your need for success is sufficiently strong to outweigh your need to be popular.' Each of these responses may be of value at different times in coaching and may take the manager towards a useful reframing of experiences.

The goal for coaches is to be conscious about their choice of response and its likely impact. Of these choices, reflecting is a useful and under utilised response that encourages managers to follow more closely their own associations, rather than those of the coach.

Normalising

Bringing emotions to the surface can feel inappropriate for managers used to maintaining a façade of logic and reason. Many are likely to view emotions as a sign of weakness, to apologise for making a fuss, and to return the conversation as quickly as possible to practical issues. However, if the coach colludes with this retreat into the safety of practical issues, the opportunity to acknowledge and make sense of these emotions will be lost. A valuable technique in the face of such retreat is normalising.

In normalising, coaches reassure managers that the feelings they are experiencing are normal. For example, a manager who is annoyed with a colleague may quickly cover over this frustration and excuse the precipitating behaviour. However, if the coach allows this frustration to be suppressed, perhaps on the basis of wanting to keep conversations constructive, then the feelings associated with the manager's handling of the colleague will be lost. On the other hand, if the coach normalises the manager's sense of frustration, enabling him or her to see it as part of the usual range of emotional responses to such circumstances, the manager can come to accept a formerly disowned aspect of his or her experience. Normalising gives managers 'permission' to have their feelings, to know their feelings, and to make space to think about how their feelings influence their thoughts and behaviours.

Externalising

It is usual in our cultural use of language to attribute traits, qualities or emotions to some fixed part of ourselves. For example, managers may make the following kinds of comments about themselves:

- 'I don't like large meetings because I am too shy.'
- 'I am very impatient if colleagues don't get things done quickly.'
- 'I avoid giving presentations because I am such an anxious person.'
- 'I get frustrated with many on the team because in contrast to them I am too competitive.'

When people internalise problematic attributes, seeing themselves variously as shy, impatient, anxious, overly competitive, or a host of other descriptions, their view of themselves becomes limited. Internalising descriptions of problematic traits reinforces the belief that there is little room for change. Once a shy person, always a shy person. Once an impatient person, always an impatient person.

Externalising is an approach to reframing problematic traits that opens up new possibilities for change (White *et al*, 1990). Rather than seeing 'the person as the problem', the aim is to recognise 'the problem as the problem'. The naming and objectifying of problematic traits places them outside the person as external factors that can be usefully managed. Externalising, as an aspect of reframing, is evoked by the particular language that coaches use in relation to managers' internalised, problematic descriptions of themselves.

Table 16 | *Internalising and externalising questions*

Internalising questions	Externalising questions
The trait 'impatient' is used as an example below. Other typical descriptions might be 'timid', 'anxious', 'competitive', 'angry', etc.	The adjective is changed to a quality described as a noun – eg 'impatience', 'timidity', 'anxiety', 'competitiveness', 'anger', etc.
• In what ways are you impatient?	• What about you allows impatience to influence your life?
• When are you impatient?	• When impatience intrudes, do you always let it take over?
• When have you regretted being impatient?	• When has impatience encouraged you to do something that you regretted later?
• What are the consequences of being impatient for your life and relationships?	• What effect does impatience have on your life and relationships?
• When do you manage not to be impatient?	• When have you resisted the intrusion of impatience?
• How do you manage not to be impatient?	• What qualities do you possess to oppose impatience?
• What are the benefits of not being impatient?	• As you stand up to impatience, what do you think you will be able to do differently?

Table 16 compares some examples of internalising and externalising questions. Internalising questions take managers' self-descriptions as givens, and in this sense can reinforce the view that a particular attribute is an unchanging part of personality.

For example, a manager who says, 'I am impatient' will be strengthened in this self-perception with questions that take this statement to be true. 'Being impatient' is viewed as a problem part of the manager. Although it may be possible to learn to control the problematic aspect, this impatient part is nevertheless viewed as something embedded within.

In contrast, externalising questions encourage managers to look afresh at their self-descriptions, distinguishing themselves from problematic emotions, thoughts and behaviours. This separation between 'the person' and 'problem stories about the person' enables managers to reframe their attitude towards themselves, questioning the degree to which an attribute is fixed, and freeing themselves up to invent new ways of being that feel authentic and useful.

For example, a manager who externalises a capacity for 'impatience' is more empowered to engage his or her internal strengths to hold the spectre of impatience at bay. The externalisation provides him or her with more space to think, and so to decide how best to handle different situations.

Making links

Making links is an important intervention at the reframing stage because it enables managers to see connections and patterns in their experiences; to be more conscious of how their feelings, thoughts and behaviours, learned through experience in relation to specific contexts, are unconsciously repeated in the present. I have already discussed many of the links that can be made between different aspects of managers' experiences, such as the different elements of managers' ACE FIRST patterns. At this stage I highlight specific considerations for making links between past and present experiences.

The first step in making links is to normalise a manager's reaction in relation to early experiences. For example, a manager may have learned, in response to a controlling and distant parent, to hide feelings of vulnerability, to over emphasise independence, and to exert control over others. The coach normalises this learning to the extent that it is viewed as a normal and healthy way of surviving emotionally within the particular context in which the manager was growing up.

However, normalising past learning is distinguished from the application of that learning in the present. Applied to present circumstances at work, the manager's distant and controlling behaviour is shown to be inappropriate and unproductive. The coach encourages the manager to distinguish between the two environmental experiences, one historical and one in the present, and to see how present behaviour has been programmed by earlier responses.

In this respect the second step in making links is to challenge the application of past learning to present work contexts.

There are thus two aspects of reframing in relation to past and present experiences. One involves the validating and normalising of the historical experience and the learning that comes from that experience. The second involves the challenging of the present-day usefulness of that learning, illustrating how it limits the manager's choices and effectiveness.

A further step in the process of making links is concerned with exploring alternative approaches to achieving results. If managers are left with a sense that their historical learning provides only a distorted view of their present reality, they will feel disabled by such links, or will ignore them in order to maintain their self-esteem.

In practice, the conscious and unconscious strategies that managers have learned for dealing with their early experiences are neither wholly effective nor wholly ineffective in relation to their present challenges, but a mixture of the two. Working to identify those areas where managers are currently most competent, coaches reinforce managers' sense that the resources for change already reside within them. The reinforcement of existing resources, and the planning of how those resources can be more widely applied to different situations, provides the basis for action plans that have a good chance of being realised.

CASE STUDY

Gordon, *continued*

According to the story that I constructed regarding Gordon's struggle to handle confrontational issues with senior colleagues, he had learned to suppress his anger as a child in the face of his father's disapproval, and was transferring this experience into the present (see Chapter 6, page 109). Although he could handle confrontation within his own team, he seemed disabled by tension amongst senior colleagues.

Making the link between his past and present experience, and using silence and reflecting to surface his emotions, he seemed struck by this insight. He realised for the first time that his behaviour with his senior colleagues bore a remarkable resemblance to how he had learned to react in the face of his father's silent criticism. He was fearful of being criticised, and since his father disapproved of showing emotion, Gordon had learned to suppress his emotions. He equated being emotional with being undignified.

In view of my construction regarding Gordon's suppressed anger, I asked him what would happen if he tried to challenge his senior colleagues. He realised that, as had occurred with his father on one occasion, he was fearful that he would become unacceptably hostile, that he would flip from withdrawn calm to uncontained anger. This was a crucial insight, because it surfaced the unconscious anger underlying his compliant style and his fear that showing such emotions would be greeted with horror.

Working with this link, I spent time normalising his mix of fear and anger as appropriate responses in the context of his father's behaviour in the past. But then I challenged the relevance of this learning to his present work experiences, where the mix of fear and suppressed anger was making him passively compliant.

By providing space for Gordon to talk about his frustrations in relation to the behaviour of his senior colleagues, his own anger was gradually diffused. This acknowledgement and working through of his feelings enabled him to think practically about a number of useful strategies to exert leadership in senior meetings, and he subsequently reported great success negotiating agreements in the face of considerable antagonism.

REFRAMING COGNITIONS

Thoughts, attitudes and beliefs (cognitions) are linked with emotions and actions within ACE FIRST patterns, and so bringing emotions to the surface inevitably leads to the identification of enabling and limiting patterns of thinking. Consequently, interventions that are designed to reframe managers' emotional experiences can be supported by interventions to reframe their cognitions.

Below, I describe three aspects of reframing in relation to cognitions – shifting perceptual position, using enabling language and using ACE records.

Shifting perceptual position

Perceptual position refers to the idea that we can look at experiences from a number of different perspectives. The importance of this idea – as noted in relation to the *focus of attention* within the ACE FIRST model – is that we can make a cognitive choice about the perceptual position that it is most useful to adopt.

Three primary perceptual positions can be differentiated:

- the *self* position
- the *other* position
- the *observer* position.

Each of these positions has potential benefits. The *self* position – experiencing events through one's own eyes – is useful for identifying goals, and for asserting oneself. The *other* position – experiencing events as if another person – is useful for empathising with others, and for motivating others. The *observer* position – experiencing events as a detached observer – is useful for encouraging objectivity, for handling emotions and for receiving difficult feedback.

Individuals vary in their bias towards one or other perceptual position, and inflexibility of perspective can represent a block to change. This can be illustrated by considering the perceptual positions that are likely to predominate for managers with a bias towards defiant or compliant leadership.

The defiant leader is more likely to view events from the self position, looking towards his or her own needs but with a limited tendency to shift to the other or observer positions. In contrast, the compliant leader is likely to view events from the other position, showing concern for the needs of others, but with a limited tendency to view events from the self or observer positions. The transactional manager (see Chapter 6, page 108) is likely to view events from the observer position, showing objectivity and reason, but with a limited tendency to view events from the self or other positions.

Getting managers to shift their perceptual position brings alternative perspectives into view – and such reflections can be a powerful basis for change.

Using enabling language

In the section on reframing emotions (above) I described the use of reflecting as a method for bringing feelings to the surface. Reflecting is also relevant in relation to thoughts and attitudes. In reflecting statements back to managers as a means of establishing empathy and acknowledgement, coaches must pay particular attention to the language they use. Certain kinds of language reinforce managers' existing assumptions about themselves, whereas small shifts in the use of language provide a subtle basis for cognitive reframing.

Table 17 contrasts reflective comments that reinforce existing frames with those that encourage reframing. Reflecting a generalisation reinforces that limiting cognition, whereas reflecting in a way that moderates or qualifies a manager's statement, invites the manager to be more precise in his or her thinking and so to consider alternative

Table 17 | *Responses that invite cognitive reframing*

Reinforcing existing frames	Reframing
GENERALISATION • You feel his behaviour shows he doesn't care about the team.	INVITING PRECISION THINKING • Some of his behaviours make you think he doesn't care about the team.
PRESUPPOSING NO CHANGE • You can't find a more suitable job for yourself.	PRESUPPOSING POSITIVE CHANGE • So you haven't found a more suitable job for yourself yet.
PRESENT PROBLEM STATEMENT • You are stressed out.	PAST PROBLEM STATEMENT • So you've been stressed out.
ACCEPTING DOUBT • You will try . . .	POSITIVE INTENTION • You will . . .
REGRET • You wish you had . . .	POSITIVE INTENTION • Next time you want to . . .
REGRET • You felt that was an awful mistake.	LEARNING • So that was a useful lesson.
PROBLEM FOCUS • So you think you are too practical to motivate others.	INTENTION FOCUS • So you'd like to motivate others more effectively.

interpretations. Managers' generalisations can be reflected and qualified in relation to amount (some/most/many), regularity (sometimes, occasionally, in that instance) and time (recently/in the past few weeks/in the last month).

For example, 'I am useless at presentations' may be reflected as 'You feel that sometimes presentations don't go well,' and 'I always end up criticising them' may be reflected as 'So in recent meetings you have ending up criticising one or two people.' Faced with such reframes, managers automatically talk with more precision.

A similar attention to the language used for reflecting can be used to reframe assumptions of no change as presuppositions of positive change, to reflect present problem statements as past problem statements, and to reflect statements that suggest doubt as statements of positive intention and learning. These linguistic reframes may seem pedantic in the ongoing flow of coaching, but if they are used persistently and respectfully, they can exert a powerful cognitive impetus for change (O'Hanlon, 1987, 1994).

Using ACE records

In making links between different elements of their experiences many managers find it useful to follow a structured process for bringing together key insights from their coaching conversations. Their cognitive understanding of how certain beliefs link with certain feelings and behaviours enables them to make sense of their characteristic ways of being. This understanding can be facilitated by drawing out some of the elements of the ACE FIRST model of change into a record that can be completed by managers in discussion with their coaches. I call this record an ACE record since its central focus is on characteristic patterns and links between *actions*, *cognitions* and *emotions* (see Table 18). However, the record also takes account of *intentions* and *results* and the degree to which the ACE pattern is effective. Finally, there is a section for recording changes that must be made in order to make the ACE pattern more effective.

In using an ACE record, managers are invited to explore the ways in which their behaviours, beliefs and emotions are either enabling or limiting them in the achievement of specific intentions. One of the benefits of using this record is that it provides explicit direction for managers to shift their *focus of attention* across the different elements of an ACE pattern. Other elements of the ACE FIRST model not included in the ACE record – the role of the *system*, and the role of *tension* in the body – also must be considered, and often contribute to the completion of an ACE record.

For example, factors relating to the system are sometimes recorded as cognitions about managers' relationships with others, and factors relating to physical tension are sometimes recorded in terms of actions that must be undertaken to reduce stress and to relax.

A worked example of the use of an ACE record is shown in the case study below.

Table 18 | *An ACE record*

INTENTION: What do you wish to achieve?	RESULT: What is the current outcome?

	ENABLING	LIMITING
ACTIONS: What behaviours do you use in relation to this intention?		
COGNITIONS: What thoughts, attitudes and beliefs about yourself or others do you have in relation to this intention?		
EMOTIONS: What feelings about yourself or others do you have in relation to this intention?		

EFFECTIVENESS: To what extent is this ACE pattern successful? (What is the gap between intentions and results?)

CHANGES: What changes do you need to make to achieve your intended results more effectively? Consider changes in actions, cognitions and emotions.

CASE STUDY

Elizabeth, *continued*

According to the story I constructed regarding Elizabeth's ability to work collaboratively with others, she defended against her fear of rejection, influenced by the early experiences of her alcoholic mother, by displaying the characteristics of defiant leadership. She was perceived as controlling, impatient and defensive with colleagues, although she could be much more considered and effective with clients.

Having explored her emotions by acknowledging and externalising her fear of making mistakes, I worked more systematically with the different elements of an ACE FIRST pattern to construct an ACE record with Elizabeth (see Table 19).

CASE STUDY continued

Table 19 | An ACE record for Elizabeth

INTENTION: To ensure that clients receive excellent service, while cultivating mutually respectful and collaborative relationships with colleagues. To get promotion onto the executive team.	RESULT: Colleagues perceive me as impatient and critical because I am determined to make sure clients get what they need. There is current doubt about my ability to work collaboratively with others.

	ENABLING	LIMITING
ACTIONS:	• Client-facing behaviours: taking time to think about the motivations of others, and listening	• Controlling • Make demands without providing a detailed brief • Appear impatient and defensive
COGNITIONS:	• 'I know how to develop excellent client relationships' • 'I can relate to people'	• 'I have higher standards than other people' • 'I do not suffer fools gladly' • 'I will be rejected if I get things wrong'
EMOTIONS:	• Optimism and enthusiasm • Concern for justice and welfare of others	• Fear of making mistakes or being considered to be incompetent • Anger and depression in the face of difficult feedback

EFFECTIVENESS:
• My current style works well with clients, but is not working with several of my senior colleagues

CHANGES:
• My controlling behaviour is driven by a fear of failure and rejection. I need to find space to think, or talk offline with someone, when I feel defensive.
• I must recognise that I am liked and valued, even when I make mistakes.
• I will apply my client-facing skills to my colleagues, listening and working out how to motivate them.
• I will play to my optimism and drive, which energises others.

We initially developed this ACE record together during Session 6, after we had already spent time building her trust, her willingness to reflect, to make links, and to acknowledge emotions. She found the process of explicitly capturing key elements of her ACE FIRST pattern very useful. She referred to it regularly in subsequent sessions as she began to cultivate more effective colleague relationships.

REFRAMING ACTIONS

The changes evoked by coaching must ultimately manifest themselves as changes in behaviour. The personal journey of coaching must be connected to the practical journey, and personal insights must be translated into new actions. In reframing actions, the coach identifies assignments, frames those assignments as experiments for managers to undertake between coaching sessions, and then reviews progress in realising changes.

Identifying assignments

I have described the shaping of intentions as containing three elements – hopes, beliefs and expectations. In reframing actions, coaches focus on the way in which the third element, shaping expectations, is realised as a commitment to take action.

Just as the story about the developmental challenges facing a manager emerges from the conversation between coach and manager, task assignments must also arise from collaborative discussion. The coach uses questioning to help managers identify assignments that require them to take actions. The coach's questioning is designed to hone broad statements of intent into sharply focused actions. For example, managers may say, 'I will delegate more,' or 'I will work on that relationship,' or 'I will make more impact in meetings.' These statements of intent are useful, but they are unlikely to be realised as change without being more sharply defined.

The process of honing assignments into precise actions is sometimes described as identifying SMART actions – actions that are Specific, Measurable, Achievable, Relevant and Time-based. However, the identification of actions is not a dry, formulaic process. Managers have to develop a picture of themselves behaving in new ways and achieving specific results. Useful questions for shaping assignments are:

- What is the first practical step you will take towards achieving that goal?
- What can you do today/tomorrow that will demonstrate that you have begun to make a change?
- If I were a fly on the wall, what would I see you doing, or hear you saying, as you undertook this new behaviour?
- How will you make this change? What strengths and skills will you draw on? What factors will make this change difficult to achieve, and how will you handle such obstacles?
- Who will be affected by your change in behaviour, and what reactions do you anticipate?
- What do you need to do to ensure that you are supported in making this change?
- How will we know if the outcome of this assignment or experiment has been successful?

Framing assignments as experiments

The purpose of an assignment is to initiate a change in behaviour, and as such, an assignment can be viewed as an experiment. The aim is for managers to explore new methods for achieving their goals, and the tailoring of these methods occurs through an iterative process of experimentation and review. Engaging a manager in an experiment is quite different from getting a person to commit to a new form of behaviour. Experimentation suggests 'having a go', whereas a commitment to a new form of behaviour can be experienced as a life sentence. If assignments are framed as experiments, managers can be encouraged to undertake the experiment without feeling obliged to adopt the new behaviour, and without trying to draw premature conclusions about its effectiveness.

Commitment to undertaking an experiment can be promoted by asking managers to describe the change in terms of an ACE FIRST pattern. What will they be *doing* differently, what will they be *thinking*, what will they be *feeling*, what *result* do they expect to achieve within that context, what physical *tension* will they be experiencing? Bringing expectations to the surface in terms of the ACE FIRST pattern encourages managers to be explicit about the difference between an old and a new pattern.

As mentioned in Chapter 1, typical experiments might include: conversations with colleagues to move the relationship forward, more effective interactions at meetings, actions to delegate more effectively, putting a case more persuasively to a team, understanding better the motivations of team members, handling a client relationship more effectively. Whatever the experiment, the coach seeks commitment that the manager will carry it out.

Commitment to change can be also reinforced by the coach's presupposition that the manager will follow through on an experiment. For example, the coach may say, 'After you do this, I want you to notice what happened, and then to describe that result to me in detail, as if I had been there, watching your experiment.' Presuppositions show that the coach really expects the experiment to be enacted. Ensuring that the assignment is written down, with a copy for the coach and the manager, further reinforces this expectation.

Reviewing progress

In terms of the LASER coaching process, reviewing progress on agreed assignments is a movement back around the cycle from *reframing* to *assessing*. In the session following the one in which a task was assigned, coaches ask managers to describe what happened in their experiments. They probe to elicit a full account of the context of the experiment, the behaviours, thoughts and feelings that were evoked, and ultimately the results that the experiment achieved. The review of assignments yields valuable information that further contributes to the coach's constructed story about managers.

If the assignment has been enacted successfully, then the coach's constructed story, and the choice of intervention, is validated. If the manager has experimented with new behaviour but the result is not successful, the coach must make sense of this outcome in terms of the ACE FIRST model of change, possibly modifying the constructed story about the manager.

For example, a manager practised the skills of delegation, and tried to put them into practice with a junior colleague. It was only through questioning about the junior colleague's dismissive response to the manager that the coach learned about how the manager's authority was being undermined by her own boss. The intentions of coaching shifted thereupon from improving delegation to one of managing upwards.

If the manager has not undertaken the assignment, the coach must make an effort to understand why. Sometimes it takes a lack of compliance on the part of a manager to demonstrate that the assignment was not sufficiently tailored to the manager's circumstances, in which case the coach and the manager discuss appropriate adjustments to the assignment. However, a lack of compliance with agreed assignments can also indicate resistance to change, and is therefore evidence that conscious or unconscious emotions must be brought to the surface and acknowledged. In this case the coach has to examine afresh the story that has been constructed about the manager, and so decide what intervention is required to acknowledge the emotions underpinning the resistance to change. This re-examination is a return to the assessing and story-making stages of the coaching process.

Even where managers have undertaken changes and achieved positive results, they may subsequently report setbacks. For example, a manager may chair a meeting more successfully than ever before as a result of coaching, but then subsequently perform less well in another meeting.

Setbacks can be very disillusioning and, if not addressed by the coach, undermine the potential for change. The idea that setbacks may occur has to be normalised as part of the process of change, and indeed valued as a positive learning experience that enables new behaviours to be refined. Anticipating setbacks and rehearsing alternative responses in the face of setbacks are important interventions for sustaining the motivation for change.

ENDING

In terms of the LASER model, ending is more a part of the learning stage than the reframing stage, since it is as part of the management of the learning space that the boundaries of coaching are established, maintained and finally terminated. Nevertheless, 'ending' is addressed here because it fits more comfortably at the end of this necessarily sequential account of the LASER coaching process.

The ending of a coaching relationship is important because its handling will determine the degree to which managers can make sustainable use of what they have learned. A coach's approach to ending the relationship parallels the approach to leadership coaching as a whole. A coaching relationship that explicitly considers personal issues and unconscious factors, as well as organisational issues, is likely to hold great significance for managers, and the prospect of ending this relationship can evoke powerful feelings. However, these feelings are not a separate consideration from the rest of coaching, but are usually a recapitulation, in a focused form, of much that has gone before. The unconscious strategies that managers apply in their relationships in life, and which have undergone examination within the coaching relationship, are precisely the strategies that tend to be re-enacted with the coach in relation to ending.

I illustrate this by considering the kinds of unconscious responses that are consistent with defiant or compliant leadership styles, and sketch useful interventions in each case. Then I consider the conscious factors that should be examined in relation to ending, and which apply to all managers, whether or not unconscious issues ought to be acknowledged first.

Unconscious emotions evoked by ending

In the case of defiant leadership, the unconscious strategy in relation to other people is one of autonomy, based on early experiences of rejection and a learned fear of dependency. For these managers, showing vulnerability is a sign of weakness. Despite insights gained through coaching about their tendency to cut off from their emotions, and the implications of this cutting off for their leadership style, these managers typically revert towards their defiant style in relation to the ending of the coaching relationship.

For example, they may propose to cancel the last couple of coaching sessions on the basis that they have learned all that they need to know already. They may revert to the transactional conversational style that was characteristic at the outset of coaching, and they may wish to focus solely on their practical goals and the evaluation of coaching.

In the case of compliant leadership, the unconscious strategy in relation to other people is one of dependency, based on early experiences of inconsistency and intrusion. For these managers, showing frustration is fraught with danger because they have a strong need to be liked. Despite insights gained through coaching about their tendency to appease others in their leadership style, these managers typically revert to their compliant style in relation to the ending of the coaching relationship.

For example, they may seek to extend the number of coaching sessions, or seek to maintain an open-ended access to the coach. They may express disproportionate gratitude to the coach, and look for approbation for their own efforts. Alternatively, they may withdraw from the interpersonal dimension by focusing on the specific procedures and expectations contained within the coaching contract, and check out that they have complied with those expectations.

Addressing the unconscious agenda

The coach's approach to these defences during ending is the same as that during other stages of coaching. The coach must manage the boundaries of the learning space, being explicit about the number of sessions that are available and the particular importance of these sessions for consolidating learning. The coach may also pre-empt the defensiveness of defiant managers by noting that it is common to withdraw or cancel sessions as a way of avoiding feelings about ending, and that in many ways these last sessions are the most important of the whole process. Alternatively, in the case of compliant managers, the coach may note that seeking to extend the contract may be a way of avoiding the feelings evoked by the ending, and that working with these feelings within the few sessions available is usually the most productive thing to do.

Having reaffirmed the boundaries of the learning space as a place to examine feelings and thoughts, as well as practical actions, the coach must acknowledge the emotions evoked by the ending, and where possible, must create links between current and past experiences. Noting a manager's withdrawal as indicative of habitual patterns of behaving in the past *and* the current work context, is a powerful (transference) interpretation. If done with compassion it can lead to a useful acknowledgement of the defiant manager's need for support, recognition and collaboration, in contrast to his or her habitual denial of dependence. On the other hand, making links between a compliant manager's desire to cling to the coaching relationship and his or her accommodating style in relation to others in the past and the present can lead to an acknowledgement of the manager's anger at having to fit in. Bringing to the surface and acknowledging these feelings, and yet not being put off by them or retaliating, the coach fosters the manager's capacity for authentic self-expression and assertiveness.

Conscious factors in relation to ending

Once unconscious feelings evoked by ending have been acknowledged, or if managers do not appear to be unduly defensive about the prospect of ending, coaches must address a number of conscious factors in relation to ending. In this area the overarching aim is to reinforce changes and to explore how those changes will be sustained.

There are a number of stages to this.

First, the coach invites managers to reflect on the degree to which personal and organisational goals have been achieved. This revisiting of goals encourages managers to consider how to maintain a creative balance between individual and organisational needs – the essence of authentic leadership.

Second, managers must identify what has changed as a result of coaching, what has enabled those changes to occur, and what is needed to maintain positive changes. If managers can identify achievements that derive from their own resources, they are more likely to draw on those resources in the future. For example, the capacity to stand back from situations and to reflect on options is a key result of coaching, and recognising this capacity encourages managers to see how they can coach themselves. Furthermore, viewing this capacity as an 'internalised coach' can reinforce their belief that they can undertake, on their own behalf, the coaching process of reflection, gaining insight and action planning.

Third, the coach and the manager must acknowledge areas where change has not occurred, and must discuss how those areas are to be managed. Sometimes initial targets for change become less important as new targets for development are identified, and so these initial areas are acknowledged as lower priorities. In other situations, managers come to realise that a desired change is unrealistic for themselves (eg in the case of a manager who prefers to be flexible and open-ended, and who yet aims to be a highly systematic project manager). In these circumstances the coach encourages managers to identify how they can work with others to manage certain aspects of their role, leaving them free to excel in their own areas of strength.

Finally, the coach and manager must revisit a number of issues that will have been agreed at the outset of coaching. If appropriate, they must agree when to book a follow-up meeting to review progress or on any further need for coaching. The coach must also confirm the process for evaluating the coaching work and get agreement that the manager will provide necessary feedback. Further, the coach must confirm the process arranged for providing the manager's boss or other sponsors with information, and check out how this is to be organised between the coach and manager.

Approaching the ending of coaching by addressing unconscious and conscious factors enables managers to internalise their learning, bringing together the multiple links and insights that they have gained, and translating these insights into sustainable strategies for improved performance.

Summary

At the reframing stage the coach makes interventions to promote change. I consider three groups of reframing interventions – those concerned with emotions, cognitions and actions. Reframing emotions is concerned with bringing emotions to the surface and acknowledging them, as the key basis for transforming them. I describe a number of techniques for working with emotions, using silence, reflecting, normalising, externalising and making links. In relation to cognitions, reframing is achieved by shifting perceptual position, using enabling language in reflecting, and by using ACE records. Acknowledgement of and clarity about emotions and cognitions paves the way for the consideration of practical actions for realising change. Reframing actions entails the identifying of assignments that require a change in behaviour, the framing of those assignments as experiments, and the reviewing of progress with those assignments in subsequent sessions.

Finally, I discuss the significance of endings in coaching, with their potential to gather together many of the key developmental issues. Paying attention to the unconscious emotions evoked by the ending, as well as explicitly reviewing and summarising areas of learning, provides the basis for sustainable change once coaching has ended.

9

Qualities and competencies

I expect I shall be a student to the end of my days.

Anton Chekhov (1860–1904)

The approach to coaching described in this book places emphasis on the need for sophistication in our approach to developing managers. On the one hand we must take account of the complexity of organisational life and the conflicting demands on managers. On the other hand we must engage with personal issues and understand how they impact on the potential of managers at work. In this chapter I examine the core competencies that coaches must have, and the types of training and experience required. Then I consider the ongoing development of coaches, and in particular the role of supervision in maintaining the quality of coaching. Finally, I turn to the issue of how sponsors can approach the buying of coaching services in a way that ensures that coaching delivers the desired results.

CORE COMPETENCIES

The behavioural skills and qualities necessary to fulfil a role can be described in terms of competencies. Although a set of competencies can never capture all of the nuances of behaviour that make a person effective within a role, they do provide a valuable method for highlighting the primary ingredients for success. The competencies identified here lay down a focus for the training and development of coaches and provide a framework against which experienced coaches can evaluate their performance. They also provide sponsors with criteria for selecting competent coaches.

I examine three core competencies for coaches:

- psychological-mindedness
- business-mindedness
- relationship development.

The presence of these three competencies ensures that coaches are able to work effectively with personal and organisational issues, and to use the relationship as the vehicle for evoking change. In my experience it is quite common to encounter coaches who have particular strength in one or two competencies but a weakness in another, and this creates lopsidedness in their coaching style.

For example, coaches who are very psychology-minded and good at relationship development, but who lack sufficient familiarity with the world of business, tend to turn coaching into counselling or psychotherapy. On the other hand, coaches who are very business-minded can lack the necessary psychology-mindedness to engage with personal issues, and so focus too exclusively on skills acquisition.

Balancing the three competencies provides the basis for coaching that evokes organisationally relevant authenticity.

Psychological-mindedness

Psychology-mindedness refers to the capacity of the coach to think about the cognitive and emotional states that underpin behaviour. In describing human behaviour we can distinguish *what* or *how* a person is doing something from considerations about *why* he or she is doing it. Whereas the *what* and the *how* of behaviour is largely open to objective verification, the *why* can never be fully known, since it asks us to consider the motivation behind behaviour. Psychological-mindedness refers to a curiosity and willingness to

Table 20 | *The coach's psychology-mindedness*

SELF-AWARENESS
Coaches demonstrate a capacity to:
• *stand back from their own experiences and notice the preferences, biases, and blind spots that underpin their behaviour*
• *give an account of their personal history, with emotional relatedness to the meaning of key events*
• *reflect on their own behaviour, and surface unconscious motivations*
• *examine their feelings, thoughts and reactions, and distinguish those evoked by others from those deriving from their own psychology (ie working with the countertransference)*
• *shift their focus of attention across different aspects of their mental and emotional experiences (eg actions, cognitions, emotions, systemic context) and entertain multiple explanations for events*
AWARENESS OF OTHERS
Coaches demonstrate a capacity to:
• *suspend judgement about a person's feelings, thoughts and behaviours*
• *evoke and build an account of a person's history, and its emotional meanings*
• *understand the conscious and unconscious motivation of others, and its affect on their thoughts and behaviour*
• *identify patterns of relating from the past that are being re-enacted in the present (ie working with the transference)*
• *make links between different domains of a person's experience (eg past/present; personal/organisational; actions, cognitions and emotions)*

engage with possible answers to the question *why?*, and to test these hypotheses through questioning and ongoing observation. In coaching, psychological-mindedness is an essential competence, since it is through constructions about underlying motives that the coach understands what factors will influence the potential for sustainable change.

Psychological-mindedness contains two similar sets of capacities – one set associated with self-awareness, and the other set associated with awareness of others (see Table 20). Self-awareness requires that coaches are reflective about their own conscious and unconscious motivations. The capacity for self-awareness is sometimes envisaged as a separation between an observing self and an experiencing self (Casement, 1985) that enables us to look objectively at our feelings, thoughts and behaviours from the outside, as well as to be experiencing them from the inside. Awareness of others derives from coaches directing the same qualities required for self-awareness to their understanding of others.

Many of the capacities contained within the concept of psychological-mindedness are part of the range of skills needed to develop the coaching relationship, and these are examined further below. However, first we must consider the coach's capacity for business-mindedness.

Business-mindedness

Coaches must be business-minded if they are to have credibility with sponsors and managers. They need to show that they understand the nature of organisational challenges, and can approach the process of coaching as a role model of business competence. To this extent I think of business-mindedness as containing two aspects (see Table 21).

First, there is the capacity of the coach to show organisational awareness. This includes being sensitive to the organisational context, understanding the structure and politics, and predicting how these will impact on a coaching assignment. Second, there is the need for the coach to handle the provision of the coaching service in a businesslike way. This includes negotiating achievable outcomes, managing boundaries, sustaining a focus on organisational goals alongside managers' personal goals, and evaluating coaching assignments effectively.

I would draw particular attention to the importance of the coach's competence at negotiating with sponsors about the purpose of coaching. This is the main opportunity coaches have for managing organisational expectations about what is achievable, and for establishing the kind of support and feedback that may be required as part of coaching. In my experience coaches can agree too readily to a piece of coaching, without consulting in depth with sponsors about the clarity and achievability of goals. In practice, sponsors value the expertise of coaches who challenge them to be realistic about the scope of coaching, and, at the end of the process, are more likely to evaluate the work objectively.

Table 21 | ***The coach's business-mindedness***

ORGANISATIONAL AWARENESS
Coaches demonstrate a capacity to:
• *understand how a business makes money; know about its products and services, its markets and competition, its financial performance and prospects*
• *comprehend how the business is structured and the nature of the key roles within the organisation*
• *identify where the power lies within an organisation, and how that power will influence a coaching assignment*
• *read the organisational context for a piece of coaching, discerning spoken and unspoken agendas*
• *discern the nature and status of key work relationships that will impact on managers' achieving their goals*
BEING BUSINESSLIKE
Coaches demonstrate a capacity to:
• *clarify and shape sponsors' goals for a piece of coaching to ensure that they are tangible and achievable*
• *manage the coaching contract, specifying and maintaining boundaries*
• *shape managers' goals and intentions so that they embrace the tension between personal and organisational goals*
• *identify practical assignments and experiments that will serve to translate insights into actions*
• *manage the evaluation of the coaching, and provide the sponsor/organisation with feedback*

Relationship development

The relationship between coach and manager is the vehicle in which all coaching occurs, and its development and management represents a key competence of the coach. Relationship development is not a wholly separate competence from psychological-mindedness and business-mindedness, but is the overarching capacity that brings these other competencies into the service of enabling change. Thus in describing the various skills associated with relationship development, I refer to various elements already highlighted within the competencies of psychological- and business-mindedness.

Productive relationships can be conceived as developing through a number of typical stages as shown in the relationship development model discussed earlier (see Chapter 6, page 106). This model of relationship development can be applied to the coaching relationship to provide an indicative picture of the various stages of its development. Figure 19 illustrates the changing focus within the coaching relationship. The vertical axis represents the extremes of results focus and relationship focus (ie intimacy). The horizontal axis represents the extremes of reinforcing trust and risking trust (ie autonomy). Five aspects to developing a coaching relationship are identified, as summarised below.

*Figure 19 | **The stages of a coaching relationship***

*Figure 19 | **The stages of a coaching relationship***

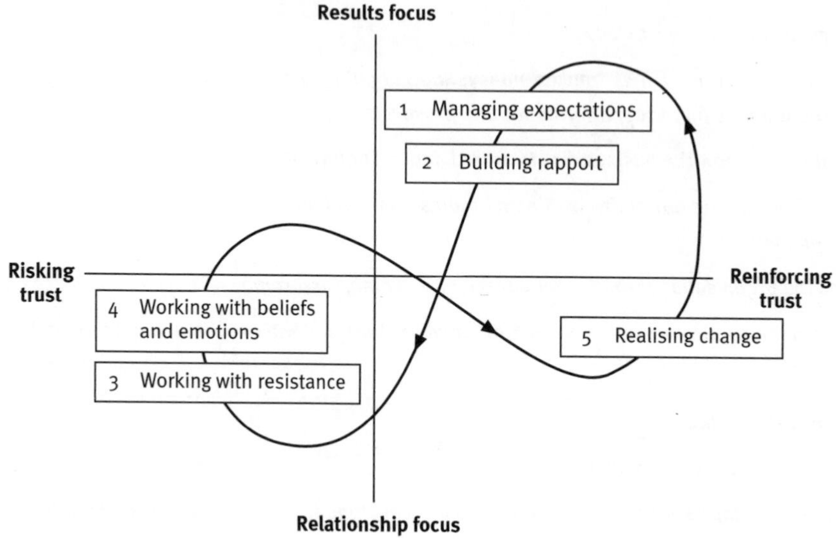

- *Managing expectations*
  Establish the purpose, expectations, boundaries and goals for coaching, from an organisational and personal perspective. Establish credibility, and contain the anxiety of managers about what coaching will entail.

- *Building rapport*
  Use active listening, questioning and reflecting to develop and demonstrate the coach's understanding of managers, paying attention to underlying motives, concerns and feelings.

- *Working with resistance*
  Make sense of conscious and unconscious blocks to change, and make useful interventions, where possible building on existing strengths and resources.

- *Working with beliefs and emotions*
  Identify, surface, acknowledge, and normalise feelings and beliefs evoked by the challenge of adopting new thoughts and behaviours, and reinforce the value of awareness and insight.

- *Realising change*
  Translate awareness and insights into practical changes in behaviour, adjusting goals and expectations if necessary, and establishing how learning will be sustained once coaching has ended.

At the outset coaches seek to 'manage expectations', and this results focus draws on their capacity for business-mindedness. Coaches ensure that personal and organisational issues are considered, and highlight the need to work with possible tensions between these agendas. Occurring in parallel with the management of expectations is 'building rapport', which draws on the capacity of coaches for psychological-mindedness. With the grounding of explicit expectations, and a sense of mutual rapport, the interactions between coaches and managers move from a results focus to a relationship focus.

Some coaches content themselves with having established this level of rapport, and back down from moving the coaching relationship on to the next two stages – that of 'working with resistance', and that of 'working with beliefs and emotions'. The difficulty in moving to these next stages is that there is a move towards 'risking trust', and coaches can be concerned that they will damage the relationship. However, it is in working with resistance that coaches make sense of managers' unconscious resistance to change, confronting and challenging blocks, providing difficult feedback, and making links about patterns of behaviour. Such challenges evoke emotions. Coaches need to work with these emotions, bringing them to the surface and acknowledging them, and enabling managers to make sense of how beliefs and feelings impact on their effectiveness.

At the stage of 'realising change', coaches encourage experimentation with new behaviours. They review goals and adjust them in view of changing organisational or personal circumstances, thereby maintaining relevance and motivation for change. Furthermore, the sense of collaboration within the relationship at this stage makes it possible for coaches and managers to review its value, to renegotiate expectations (returning to Stage 1), and to establish how learning will be sustained once coaching has ended.

TRAINING

As the demand for coaching has grown, many people offer themselves as coaches to organisations. However, the training and experience of coaches varies enormously, and without any established consensus about the requirements for coaches, sponsors are forced to make judgements about who to use. Many coaches offer their services on the basis of having been a manager within an organisation. Other coaches are qualified counsellors or psychotherapists who offer their clinical training and experience as evidence of their capacity to develop others. Yet other coaches typically have an experience in the provision of training, consultancy, psychology, or education. Although many of these coaches may be highly skilled within certain areas, they must develop a *blend* of skills to be more effective.

The specific training of coaches is in its infancy. The last few years has seen the introduction of a number of academic courses in coaching and mentoring, and others are likely to come on stream in the near future. To develop the appropriate blend of skills for coaching, such courses must cover the three core competencies discussed above, and provide opportunities for theoretical and experiential learning in each of these areas (see Figure 20).

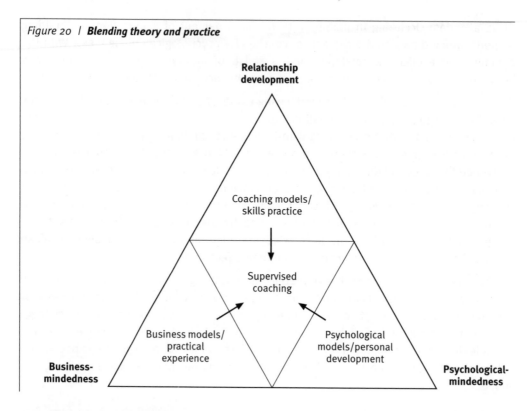

Figure 20 | Blending theory and practice

THEORETICAL LEARNING

Theoretical learning must cover the three core competencies – those of psychology, business and coaching. I outline some of the key areas of theory with which coaches have to be familiar.

Psychological models

From the perspective of psychology, coaches must have an understanding of some of the major psychological models, since these provide useful frameworks for making sense of many of the personal challenges that face managers. They include models of learning, development, personality and motivation. In addition, coaches must have a grasp of one or more of the major schools of psychotherapy, such as psychoanalysis, cognitive-behavioural, Gestalt, humanistic, or systemic psychotherapy. These theories and models provide the conceptual basis for the application of psychological-mindedness.

Business models

From the perspective of business, coaches must have an understanding of organisational context, including culture, structure and strategy. Further, they must be able to make sense of the behaviour of individuals in organisations in terms of models of leadership, management and team development. Coaches must also understand the way that roles and responsibilities for a job are constructed, and how the performance of managers is measured and managed. These theories and models, supported by illustrative case studies, provide the conceptual grounding for the application of business-mindedness.

Coaching models

As coaching within organisations matures as a discipline it is gradually defining its own body of theory, distinct from that of psychology or business. Thus coaches' conceptual understanding must include models of individual change within organisations, and an understanding of the psychometric instruments used for development. A grasp of different models of consulting enables coaches to distinguish solution- and process-oriented approaches, and to identify the key listening and questioning skills that underpin the development of effective relationships with sponsors and managers. Within this area coaches must also understand how to manage the contract and boundaries of coaching, and how to collect and provide feedback on outcomes. These conceptual frameworks provide the basis for what I have described as relationship development within an organisational context.

EXPERIENTIAL LEARNING

Coaches cannot be effective without a rich and varied range of experience under their belts. As with theoretical learning, experiential learning can be linked with each of the core competencies for coaching. Coaches thus need experiences that cultivate psychological-mindedness, business-mindedness and relationship development.

Personal development

In terms of psychological-mindedness, the most important learning experience comes from coaches themselves receiving some form of one-to-one development. At the heart of psychological-mindedness is the capacity for self-awareness, and this can only be achieved by coaches' submitting themselves to an extended and concentrated process of self-reflection. Such self-reflection and examination can, to some extent, be obtained from personal development workshops, psychometric tests and feedback from others within reflective learning sets, particularly if those providing feedback are themselves psychologically mature and interpersonally skilled. However, in my view coaches need to 'walk the talk' and to undergo their own one-to-one development within coaching, counselling or psychotherapy.

The particular brand of personal development will depend on the preference of the individual, but in my view coaches need to undergo at least 12 months of one-to-one development, and more if they expect to work with managers for an extended period. The logic of this view is that coaches must be more self-aware than the managers with whom they will be working. Although the length of time that someone undertakes personal work is no guarantee of self-awareness, this approach does ensure that coaches engage with their personal issues.

Furthermore, the type of one-to-one development has to be at least as 'deep' as the kind they wish to offer. For example, if coaches want to work with unconscious issues, they must undertake personal work that engages with their own unconscious motivations.

Business experience

Many coaches have prior experience of working within organisations, perhaps as a manager, trainer, or even board director, and this practical knowledge of organisational life is invaluable for enabling coaches to understand the tasks, issues and frustrations of those they are coaching. The common challenges of working in organisations, of exerting influence across a network of decision-makers, of motivating others, of keeping focused on key priorities, of meeting targets within defined budgets – these are the kinds of realities that are best understood by those who have had to grapple with them.

Coaches must gain exposure to the workings of organisations, and if they have not had direct experience from within organisations, they must undertake assignments or projects that encourage them to appreciate the complexity of enabling change within an organisational context. Some practical experience of organisational life – particularly for those who have a background in counselling, for example – encourages coaches to consider the systemic context in which their work is taking place, and alerts them to the need to construct realistic goals that embrace personal and organisational issues.

Skills practice in relationship development

There are a number of interpersonal skills that are essential to the development of one-to-one relationships. These include active listening, questioning, empathising, challenging, demonstrating understanding, synthesising ideas and providing feedback. Such skills are common to a range of courses on topics like negotiating, counselling, consulting, managing others, as well as coaching, and they can be usefully practised as role-plays on a training course. Typically, participants work in groups of three, in which one person takes the role of the coach, one the role of the manager and the third person takes the role of the objective observer.

In such role-plays the coach practises the use of a range of skills designed to uncover the manager's issues, and to develop the trust and collaboration with the manager. Whether captured on video or simply reviewed in discussion after the role-play, this kind of practice readily reveals strengths and weaknesses, and provides targets for skills development.

Supervised coaching as part of training

Ultimately those undertaking training in coaching must apply their theoretical and experiential learning to the practice of doing coaching. I examine below the role of supervision as an essential requirement for all coaches, whether trainees or experienced coaches. For trainees, the supervision of their work by an experienced coach provides a reflective space for bringing together theory and practice. In a training supervision, coaches give an account of a session, identifying the issues they are working on, and their options on how to move the process of coaching forward. Discussed in one-to-one or group supervision, the coach is given the opportunity to reflect on his or her approach. This reflective space, which is in many respects a mirror of the learning space provided by coaches for managers, encourages coaches to examine different constructions and scenarios, to evaluate their use of key skills, and to entertain different possible interventions. Importantly, supervision also provides coaches with feedback about their own blind spots, and so yields useful information for further developing self-awareness.

ONGOING DEVELOPMENT

Practitioners in all fields need to maintain and expand their skills, and this is no less the case for coaches. Coaches must ensure that their psychological and business skills are kept current through continuing professional development. This typically includes attending conferences, going on courses, reading, and in some cases, making use of a personal coach, counsellor or psychotherapist. However, the most important element of ongoing development for coaches is the use of consultative supervision.

Supervision

The concept of supervision as an ongoing method for maintaining the quality of coaching has evolved from the fields of counselling and psychotherapy, in which experienced practitioners reflect on their work in individual, group, or peer supervision (Gilbert *et al*, 2000). In the disciplines of coaching and other forms of one-to-one development, effectiveness is dependent on the capacity of coaches to attend to the process of interactions, as well as the content of their discussions. The problem with any discipline that involves the examination of process is that if a person is inside the process, it can be very difficult to see what is going on.

In discussing the role of self-awareness as part of the psychological-mindedness of the coach, I have distinguished between an 'observing' and an 'experiencing' part of the self. It is the coach's capacity to move towards the 'observing' part of the self that provides the essential distance for reflection, awareness and insight. However, when coaches enter into the manager's world and system, it can be very difficult to sustain an observer perspective. They can find themselves unconsciously caught up in the agendas of the organisation and the interpersonal patterns of managers. Without a method for stepping outside the experience, for examining their own potential blind spots, coaches will inevitably replicate unconscious or unspoken patterns.

Supervision provides a space to reflect. It re-establishes and reinforces the coach's capacity for observing as well as experiencing. In conversations with a supervisor, coaches examine how their reactions and responses are unconsciously shaped, most directly by managers, and more distantly by the system in which the manager operates. These reflective conversations enable coaches to move between different perspectives, sometimes experiencing their own reactions to an organisation or manager, and sometimes stepping outside these experiences to make sense of them.

The essential value of this reflective process derives from the fact that the success of coaching can depend on the coach's understanding of unconscious issues.

First, there are the unconscious issues of the manager. In this case supervision helps coaches to verbalise and make sense of these issues, and to decide whether they are qualified to handle them. If coaches are sufficiently psychologically-minded, they can use supervision to understand how to work with these unconscious factors. If, on the other hand, it becomes apparent that coaches are not qualified to deal with the issues that are surfacing, supervision helps them both to realise this and to think through how to encourage managers to consult with other professionals.

Second, quite apart from whether coaches are sufficiently qualified, their own unconscious issues can also cause problems. Supervision provides a space specifically designed to increase the self-awareness of coaches, and for them to understand how they may be unconsciously responding to the client. This aspect of reflection may reveal learning issues and blind spots in the coach which, if not acknowledged, will undermine the coaching outcome. On the other hand, this reflection may reveal reactions that help the coach to make sense of the manager's unconscious experience, and in this way provide an experiential basis for insight into facilitating change. (See the sections on countertransference as intrusion or indicator, pages 89–90.)

A final point to make in relation to supervision concerns the necessary qualifications and experience of supervisors. In my view supervisors should be able to demonstrate competence and a depth of experience in each of the areas of psychology-mindedness, business-mindedness and relationship development. Furthermore, in view of the particular emphasis on reflection and the need to work with unconscious issues in supervision, supervisors will often benefit from an extended piece of personal coaching, counselling or psychotherapy, as well as training as a psychodynamic counsellor or psychotherapist.

BUYING COACHING

Sponsors of coaching in organisations, usually either human resource professionals or line managers, play a central role in setting the standards for the quality of coaching, since it is in the context of their expectations that the provision of coaching develops. If coaching is to become more sophisticated and to provide managers with a more profound developmental experience, sponsors have to understand how to buy coaching services that address the need for authentic leadership within their organisations. The sophistication of sponsors in their attitudes to coaching will thus have a direct impact on the sophistication of coaches.

Currently, many coaches are appointed to work with managers who have insufficient training or experience to engage with the complexity of facilitating fundamental change. Higher expectations from sponsors, reinforced by selection criteria for coaches, will encourage prospective coaches to undertake more systematic personal development, and to extend their capacity to evoke change.

The main method by which sponsors set standards in coaching is in their purchase of external coaching services. Furthermore, their effective buying and management of the process of coaching ensures that their organisation, and their managers, accrue real value from the investment in coaching. Sponsors must therefore approach the buying of coaching in a systematic way.

I propose a four-stage process for buying coaching:[1]

- Identify the individual and organisational purpose.
- Assess the development challenge.
- Select an appropriately qualified and experienced coach.
- Manage the process.

Below, I examine the issues that sponsors must consider at each of these stages.

Identify the individual and organisational purpose

The first step in the process of buying coaching is to consider its purpose. A key question that sponsors should ask themselves is:

- 'How will we know if coaching has been successful for the manager(s) and the organisation?'

This question forces sponsors to think practically about the purpose of coaching. Although it may be too ambitious to expect coaching alone to secure widescale organisational change, identifying broader organisational goals to which coaching is intended to contribute helps sponsors and coaches to shape the purpose of coaching in business terms. In particular, it challenges them to construct development objectives for managers that are explicitly linked to organisational objectives.

For example, there may be an organisational intention to measurably improve the productivity of a department. This organisational objective can be linked to a manager's coaching objectives, which may be to manage a team more effectively, both by being more assertive about performance standards, and by being more motivational in the assignment of work. Linking individual goals to broader organisational objectives, sponsors are challenged to think practically about the desirable endpoints of coaching, and to be realistic about what is achievable.

It is also important for sponsors to consider the potential value of coaching to the organisation, and to this end they must consider the degree to which managers being considered for coaching shape or influence the business. This does not mean that coaching should be offered only to those in the most senior leadership positions with responsibility for organisational strategy. There are many others – perhaps in team leadership, project management, or client relationship roles, for example – who can have a profound impact on the success of the organisation, and who are potential candidates for coaching. This consideration of the current and future potential of managers encourages sponsors to target coaching primarily on those who can make a significant contribution to the business in the short to mid-term.

If managers are derailing in their role, sponsors have to question the value of using coaching resources to evoke change. There are some exceptions, such as managers who have shown real potential in the past and who need to be supported through a difficult patch, or managers who have rare strengths that need to be accommodated as much as possible to the organisation. But generally the use of coaching for derailing managers represents an ineffective use of resources. Although the organisation may choose to support such managers in helping them to decide on alternative career choices, this kind of support should be distinguished from leadership coaching for high-potential managers.

In assessing the purpose of coaching, sponsors must also consider the degree to which the organisation can get real value from coaching if it is provided on an ad hoc basis for individuals. In my experience programmes of coaching for a cohort of selected managers, either within a department or across a range of departments, can represent a very effective method for achieving individual and organisational change. The fact that the coaching sits within a programme means that organisational goals can be identified that are consistent across all managers, while the realisation of these organisational goals can be explored at an individual level within the tailored process of one-to-one coaching. Furthermore, the evaluation of such coaching programmes provides the organisation with valuable information about the capabilities of groups of high-potential managers, and can further inform its human resource strategy.

Assess the development challenge

The second step in the process of buying coaching is to assess the development challenge that faces managers. Key questions for the sponsor to consider are:

- What is the nature of the change the person or people need(s) to undertake?
- To what extent will the desired change involve a challenge to how a person behaves or interacts?

Sponsors must consider the degree to which development will require an engagement with the personal as well as the practical aspects of change. This is difficult to know, because in effect it is asking the sponsor to make a judgement about a manager's psychological readiness to change. If all coaches displayed psychological-mindedness and business-mindedness in equal measure, then sponsors could afford to be less concerned with this issue, since they could rely on the coach to respond flexibly to the development challenges as they surfaced within the process of coaching. However, in practice coaches have strengths and weaknesses, and different experiences equip them better for different coaching challenges.

A useful distinction for sponsors to consider is the distinction between two types of learning – receptive learning and reflective learning.[2] *Receptive learning* is the receiving of knowledge from outside. In this case a coach imparts wisdom or advice, suggests how to use new skills, and provides one-to-one training. *Reflective learning* is the integration of personal motivations and styles with external needs and knowledge. The coach encourages self- and interpersonal awareness in relation to an individual's role, goals and behaviours.

From an organisational perspective, sponsors can be reactively drawn towards coaching as an opportunity to evoke receptive learning, since their primary goal is to see managers adopt new behaviours and to be more effective. Where managers are open and motivated to learn, and where there are prescribed skills and solutions that can be readily absorbed through conversation, coaching that evokes receptive learning can be effective. However, such an approach to coaching tends to *impose* knowledge, and can fail to help managers assimilate the learning, or to respond to it with personal creativity and authenticity.

Reflective learning of the kind described in this book encourages managers to look inside, to understand their aspirations, strengths and issues, and how they impact on their capacity to achieve their personal and organisational goals. The great benefit of linking personal and organisational agendas is that it engages the motivation and authenticity of managers. However, organisations can be uncomfortable sponsoring this kind of learning because it may take longer than receptive learning, and it may stir up personal issues that are considered inappropriate within an organisational setting.

In my experience sponsors' judgements about the nature of the learning challenge, and the kind of learning that they wish coaching to evoke, is strongly biased by their personal preferences in relation to learning. Those who adopt a pragmatic and no-nonsense approach to their own learning typically view managers' development challenges in terms of the need to acquire new skills, and see coaching as a means for evoking receptive learning. On the other hand, those who prefer to reflect deeply about themselves typically view managers' development challenges in terms of the need to increase awareness and insight, and regard coaching as an opportunity to evoke reflective learning. The more self-aware that sponsors are of their own biases, the more able they are to make objective judgements about the nature of the development challenge facing managers, and the degree to which coaching should evoke receptive or reflective learning.

Some sponsors recognise that they are not qualified to diagnose the nature of the development challenges facing managers, and so prefer to use a business psychologist or experienced coach to provide an initial assessment. Such assessments can be very useful for helping managers to understand more clearly what they wish to get out of coaching, and provide sponsors with an explicit recommendation on the kind of expertise a coach will need.

Select a coach

The third step in the process of buying coaching is to select an appropriately qualified and experienced coach. The selection of a coach is directly linked to the earlier assessment of the development challenge facing managers. The key questions that sponsors ought to consider are:

- To what extent are there coaches available who provide the full blend of psychological-mindedness, business-mindedness and relationship development?
- If it is necessary to make a trade-off between business relevance and psychological competence, which is the more important capability for this manager?

Ideally, sponsors select a coach who can provide directly relevant business experience as well as a depth of expertise in coaching, in which case the coach is able to offer receptive and reflective learning. However, in practice, sponsors often need to make a trade-off between the relevance of a coach's business experience and his or her competence at working with personal issues.

Where the required learning is primarily receptive learning – perhaps because the manager is well motivated and primarily needs to acquire new skills – it is appropriate to select a coach who can be a skills expert and role model (see Table 22). In this case the coach is typically a person whose business experience is directly relevant, perhaps having worked in the same industry as the manager, and perhaps also having fulfilled the same role as the manager in the past. This kind of coach corresponds to the traditional definition of a mentor as an experienced and trusted adviser.

Where the required learning is to evolve out of a process of reflection – perhaps because the manager needs to identify core motivations and to connect these to more effective patterns of behaviour – it is appropriate to select a coach who can be an enabler of individual potential. In this case the coach is typically a person who has a blend of the core competencies described above, but whose business experience may not be so directly relevant to that of the manager. As long as the coach has sufficient business knowledge to be able to empathise with the realities and challenges of the manager's role, this lack of directly relevant business experience need not be a problem. Indeed, it could be argued that in many circumstances it is better that the coach is *not* an expert in the manager's job, because such knowledge would inevitably lead to the coach's making assumptions about the manager's role rather than adopting an attitude of open inquiry.

Table 22 | The skills expert and the enabler

The coach as skills expert	The coach as enabler
PURPOSE • *To impart specific knowledge and skills* • *To examine manifest strengths and weaknesses* • *To help managers to handle situations more effectively, drawing on the coach's experience* *REQUIREMENTS* • *Relevant expertise and experience of the manager's industry, organisation and functional role* • *An encouraging and motivational interpersonal style*	*PURPOSE* • *To facilitate self-awareness and insight as the foundation for change* • *To build self-belief, confidence and interpersonal competence* • *To link individual authenticity to the practical achievement of organisational goals* *REQUIREMENTS* • *Evidence of psychological-mindedness, business-mindedness and relationship development* • *The capacity to translate insights into practical change*

Manage the process

The fourth step in buying coaching is to manage the process. The role of the sponsor in managing the coaching process can significantly influence its success. At the outset the sponsor is responsible for identifying and understanding the need for coaching, and for assessing the openness of managers to receiving coaching. If managers are uncertain or reluctant, sponsors must understand the context for their resistance, and reassure them about the boundaries, confidentiality and expectations of coaching. Furthermore, if the sponsor is a human resource manager, he or she must discuss the goals of coaching with the manager's boss, and establish realistic expectations with the boss about what can be achieved and what they need to do to support the process.

The sponsor must consider the development challenges for managers and make a decision on the kind of coach that is required. Prospective coaches should be expected to provide written confirmation of their training, experience and qualifications, including references from coaching assignments that they have undertaken. The sponsor should look for evidence of psychological-mindedness, business-mindedness, relationship development and information about continuing professional development, particularly ongoing supervision.

Increasingly, there are organisations that specialise in coaching, which are usually willing to provide details of the credentials of all of their coaches, and to discuss with the sponsor which coaches may be suitable for particular managers. If the sponsor is making the selection, the reviewing of credentials and thereafter meeting with the coaches should put the sponsor in a position to make a selection. If managers are to choose the coach for themselves, the sponsor can be a useful sounding-board for helping them think through the pros and cons of different coaches.

The sponsor is often responsible for the initial briefing to a coach, and at this briefing he or she should expect to provide full information about the organisational context and objectives for the coaching assignment and, if appropriate, some information about the particular development challenges facing the manager. There should also be discussion of the coaching contract, including costs, the number and length of sessions, the handling of cancellations, the handling of confidentiality, the way in which feedback is to be provided for the organisation, and the way in which the work is to be evaluated. If 360-degree feedback or psychometric tools are to be used, the sponsor should establish how this process will work, and what information will be made available to the organisation.

Sponsors must also agree the way in which coaching is to be reviewed and evaluated, and be explicit about the kinds of output that are expected from coaching conversations. Typically, managers agree to provide a summary of the ongoing development goals that they have identified in coaching, and to report these to their boss. Alternatively, they agree with the coach what information will be fed back to their boss, which is then either done as a three-way meeting between coach, manager and boss, or directly by the coach with the boss.

Where coaching has been undertaken as part of a programme with a number of managers, sponsors should expect the coach or coaching organisation to provide a summary of the development themes, without attributing these to individual managers. Such information can be very useful for providing insight into the capabilities of managers in the organisation.

Finally, the sponsor must provide the coach with feedback about the process and outcomes of the work, identifying those aspects that need to be improved on future assignments, and highlighting those aspects of the coaching process that have been most effective.

Summary

Coaches must fulfil certain requirements if they are to engage with managers' personal and organisational issues and to evoke their capacity for authentic leadership. Three core competencies for coaches are identified – psychological-mindedness, business-mindedness, and relationship development. These core competencies can be developed through a mix of theoretical and experiential learning. Coaches must also undertake ongoing development, and in particular need to be supervised, since supervision provides the essential reflective space necessary for them to observe their own unconscious patterns and reactions.

Finally, a four-stage process for buying coaching services is proposed for sponsors. These stages are: identifying the individual and organisational purpose of coaching, assessing the development challenge, selecting an appropriately qualified and experienced coach, and managing the overall coaching process on behalf of the organisation. It is the effective management of this process by sponsors that helps to raise the standards of coaching available to managers in organisations.

ENDNOTES

1 This process was developed in discussion with my coaching colleague Liz Pick.
2 The distinction between receptive and reflective learning is intended to be a more accessible way of talking about single-loop and double-loop learning (see C. Argyris, *Reason, Learning and Action* (1982) San Francisco, Jossey Bass).

References and further reading

AINSWORTH, M. (1982) 'Attachment: retrospect and prospect', in Parkes, C. M. *and* Stevenson-Hinde, J. *The Place of Attachment in Human Behaviour*. London, Routledge.

ARGYRIS, C. (1982) *Reason, Learning and Action*. San Francisco, Jossey Bass.

BERGLAS, S. (2002) 'The very real dangers of executive coaching', *Harvard Business Review*, June: 87–92.

BERK, M. S. *and* ANDERSEN, S. M. (forthcoming) 'The impact of past relationships on interpersonal behaviour: Behavioural confirmation in the social-cognitive process of transference', *Journal of Social Psychology*.

BION, W. R. (1961) *Experiences in Groups*. London, Tavistock.

BION, W. (1962) *Learning from Experience*. London, Heinemann.

BION, W. (1970) *Attention and Interpretation*. London, Karnac.

BOWLBY, J. A. (1988) *Secure Base: Clinical applications of attachment theory*. London, Tavistock/Routledge.

BREWIN, C. R. *and* ANDREWS, B. (2000) 'Psychological defence mechanisms: the example of repression', *The Psychologist*, Vol. 13, No. 12, December: 615–617.

CASEMENT, P. (1985) *On Learning from the Patient*. London, Routledge.

CHEN, S. *and* ANDERSEN, S. M. (1999) 'Relationships from the past in the present: Significant-other representations and transference in interpersonal life', in Zanna, M. P. (ed.) *Advances in Experimental Social Psychology*. Vol. 31: 123–190. San Diego, CA, Academic Press.

CHEKHOV, A. (1904) *The Cherry Orchard*, Act 1.

CIOFFI, F. (1970) 'Freud and the idea of pseudo-science', in Borger, R. and Cioffi, F. (eds) *Explanations in the Behavioural Sciences*. Cambridge, CUP.

COVEY, S. R. (1989) *The Seven Habits of Highly Effective People: Powerful lessons in personal change*. London, Simon & Schuster.

CRIBBS, G. (2002) 'The perils of choosing the right business coach', *Financial Times*, 2 December: 15.

DALLOS, R. *and* DRAPER, R. (2000) *An Introduction to Family Therapy: Systemic theory and practice*. Buckingham, Open University Press.

DARWIN, C. 'I must begin . . .' Letter to J. Fiske, 6 December 1874.

Digman, J. M. (1990) 'Personality structure: emergence of the five-factor model', *Annual Review of Psychology*, No. 41: 417–440.

Eaves, L., Eysenck, H. J. and Martin, N. G. (1989) *Genes, Culture, and Personality*. New York, Academic.

Ekman, P. (1986) *Telling Lies*. New York, Berkley Books.

Ellenberger, H. F. (1970) *The Discovery of the Unconscious: The history and evolution of dynamic psychiatry*. New York, Basic Books.

Ewen, R. B. (1998) *Personality: A topical approach*. Mahweh, NJ, Erlbaum.

Fonagy, P. (1993) 'Psychoanalytic and empirical approaches to developmental psychopathology: Can they be usefully integrated?', *Journal of the Royal Society of Medicine*, 86: 577–581.

Freud, S. (1960) *The Psychopathology of Everyday Life*. Harmondsworth, Penguin. [Original work published 1914.]

Freud, S. (1984) 'The unconscious', in Richards, A. (ed.) The Pelican Freud Library, Vol 11. *On Metapsychology: The theory of psychoanalysis* (159–222). Harmondsworth, Penguin. [Original work published 1915.]

Freud, S. (1922) *Introductory Lectures on Psychoanalysis*. London, George Allen & Unwin.

Freud, S. 'The poets and philosophers . . .' Remark on his 70th birthday. Quoted in Trilling, L. (1957) *The Liberal Imagination*.

Gergen, K. (1985) 'The Social Constructionist Movement in modern psychology', *American Psychologist*, No. 40: 266–275.

Gilbert, M. C. and Evans, K. (2000) *Psychotherapy Supervision*. Buckingham, Open University Press.

Glassman, N. S. and Andersen, S. M. (1999) 'Activating transference without consciousness: Using significant-other representations to go beyond what is subliminally given', *Journal of Personality and Social Psychology*, No. 77: 1146–1162.

Goleman, D. (1996) *Emotional Intelligence: Why it can matter more than IQ*. London, Bloomsbury.

Greenberg, J. R. and Mitchell, S. A. (1983) *Object Relations in Psychoanalytic Theory*. Cambridge, Massachusetts, Harvard University Press.

Greenberger, D. and Padesky, C. A. (1995) *Mind Over Mood: Change how you feel by changing the way you think*. London, Guildford Press.

Hinkley, K. and Andersen, S. M. (1996) 'The working self-concept in transference: Significant-other activation and self change', *Journal of Personality and Social Psychology*, No. 71: 1279–1295.

Hinshelwood, R. D. (1991) *A Dictionary of Kleinian Thought*. London, Free Association Books.

Hirschhorn, L. (1993) *The Workplace Within*, 5th edition. London, MIT Press.

Holmes, J. (1996) *Attachment, Intimacy, Autonomy: Using attachment theory in adult psychotherapy*. London, Jason Aronson.

Jung, C. G. (1971) *Psychological Types*. Bollingen Series XX. The Collected Works of C. G. Jung (Vol. 6). Princeton, NJ, Princeton University Press.

Kagan, J. (1994) *Galan's Prophecy*. New York, Basic Books.

KIERKEGAARD, S. (1844) *Philosophical Fragments.*

KLEIN, M. (1988) 'Notes on some schizoid mechanisms', in *Envy and Gratitude and Other Works.* London, Hogarth.

LEE, G. (1997) 'Alone among three', in RICHARDS, V. (ed.) *Fathers, Families, and the Outside World.* London, Karnac.

LEE, G. (2001) 'The relationship dimension in management development', *Organisations and People*, Vol. 8, No 3: 32–40.

LOCKE, J. (1690) *An Essay in Human Understanding.* Book 4. .

LOFTUS, M. (2000) *Guide to the Relationship Q.* Oxford, OCG Limited.

LOEHLIN, J. C. (1992) *Genes and Environment in Personality Development.* Newberry Park, California, Sage.

MEDAWAR, P. B. (1975) 'Victims of psychiatry', in *The New York Review of Books*, 22 January. Cited in Jahoda, M. (1977) *Freud and the Dilemmas of Psychology.* London, Hogarth.

MENZIES, I. (1975) 'A case study in the functioning of social systems as a defense against anxiety', in Coleman, A *and* Bexton, W. H. (eds) *Group Relations Reader.* Sausalito, CA, Grex: 281–312.

OGDEN, T. H. (1986) *The Matrix of Mind.* London, Karnac.

O'HANLON, W. H. (1987) *Taproots: Underlying principles of Milton Erickson's therapy and hypnosis.* New York, Norton.

O'HANLON, W. H. *and* WILK, J. (1987) *Shifting Contexts: The generation of effective psychotherapy.* New York, Guildford.

O'HANLON, W. H. *and* BEADLE, A. (1994) *A Field Guide to PossibilityLand: Possibility therapy methods.* Omaha: Possibility Press.

PADESKY, C. A. *and* GREENBERGER, D. (1995) *A Clinician's Guide to Mind Over Mood.* London, Guildford Press.

PINE, M. (1990) *Drive, Ego, Object and Self: A synthesis for clinical work.* New York, Basic Books.

PLOMIN, R. (1994) *Genetics and Experience: The interplay between nature and nurture.* Thousand Oaks, Sage.

POWER, M. J. (1997) 'Conscious and unconscious representations of meaning', in POWER, M. J. *and* BREWIN, C. R. (eds) *The Transformation of Meaning in Psychological Therapies.* Chichester, Wiley.

POWER, M. (2000) 'Freud and the unconscious', *The Psychologist*, Vol. 13, No. 12, December: 612–614.

PROUST, M. (1913–1927) *À la Recherche du Temps Perdu.*

ROGERS, C. R. (1961) *On Becoming a Person.* London, Constable.

ROGERS, C. R. *and* STEVENS, B. (eds) (1967) *Person to Person: The problem of being human.* Moab, Utah, Real People Press.

ROLLINS, H. E. (ed.) (1972) *The Letters of John Keats*, Vol. 1. Cambridge, MA, Harvard University Press: 193.

SALOVEY, P. *and* MAYER, J. D. (1990) *Emotional Intelligence: Imagination, cognition and personality*, No 9: 185–211.

SZAZ, T. (1962) *The Myth of Mental Illness.* London, Secker & Warburg.

Tarvis, C. (1989) *Anger: The misunderstood emotion*. New York, Touchstone.

Wales, S. (2003) 'Why coaching?', *Journal of Change Management*, Vol. 3, No. 3, February: 275–282.

Weiskrantz, L. (1997) *Consciousness Lost and Found: A neuropsychological exploration*. Oxford, Oxford University Press.

White, M. *and* Epston, D. (1990) *Narrative Means to Therapeutic Ends*. New York, Norton.

Williams, D. I. *and* Irving, J. A. (2001) 'Coaching: an unregulated, unstructured and (potentially) unethical process', *Occupational Psychologist*, No. 42, April: 3–7.

Winnicott, D. W. (1971) *Playing and Reality*. London, Tavistock.

Index

Membership has its rewards

Join us online today as an Affiliate member and get immediate access to our member services. As a member you'll also be entitled to special discounts on our range of courses, conferences, books and training resources.

To find out more, visit www.cipd.co.uk/affiliate or call us on 020 8612 6208.

The Coach's Coach

Personal development for personal developers

Alison Hardingham

with Mike Brearley, Adrian Moorhouse and Brendan Venter

Being a coach is a tricky job, so whether you are an experienced coach or just starting out; a specialist consultant or a coaching manager, this book will help you become better and enjoy coaching more. It will help you to help the people you are coaching improve their performance – which, after all, is why you became a coach in the first place.

Alison Hardingham is a successful business coach and offers advice, techniques and examples drawn from experience of coaching people in all kinds of organisations and with the contributions of three phenomenally successful sports people: Mike Brearley, Adrian Moorhouse and Brendan Venter, you will be on track to being 'coach of the year'.

Mike Brearly is one of England's best known and most successful cricket captain; **Adrian Moorhouse** broke the world record in breast stroke five times and won an Olympic gold medal; and **Brendan Venter** was a member of the Springboks, South African Rugby Team, and subsequently played and coached at London Irish.

Order your copy now by visiting us online at www.cipd.co.uk/bookstore or call us on 0870 800 3366

Alison Hardingham is a business psychologist with more than twenty years' experience of coaching individuals and teams. She is a successful author and conference speaker.

| 2004 | 1 84398 075 4 | Paperback | 216 pages |

The Chartered Institute of Personnel and Development is the leading publisher of books and reports for personnel and training professionals, students, and for all those concerned with the effective management and development of people at work.